YOGA FOR HEALTH

by

Avadhutika Anandamitra Acarya

Ananda Marga Publications
Singapore • Manila • Jakarta • Malaysia • Thailand

Published and Distributed by:

Ananda Marga Publications
1278 Syson St. Paco, Manila
1007 Philippines
Tel. 58-22-15
Fax 521-4963

Singapore
Ananda Marga Publications
715 Upper Changi Rd. East
Singapore 1648
Tels. 542-7153/545-7014
Fax 542-7153

Malaysia
Ananda Marga Publications
c/o Apple house
1F, Jln. Sungai Kelian
Tanjong Bungah
11200 Penang, Malaysia
Tel. 80-42-62

Indonesia
Ananda Marga Publications
Tanjung Duren Utara 9/17
Jakarta Barat, Indonesia
Tel. 51-34-40

Thailand
Ananda Marga Publications
130, Soi 36, Ramkhamhaeng
Bangkok, Thailand
Tel. 375-1608

Printed by: Ocean Colour Printing Pte. Ltd. (S'pore)

ISBN 971-8623-01-9

CONTENTS

Illness and the Mind

"Very few people know what real health is because most are occupied with killing themselves slowly. . .the body must be in an intimate relationship with the mind."[1]

Albert Szent-Gyorgi, scientist

All over the world today, in matters of health and healing, a profound change has suddenly started to occur. Doctors are realizing that the onset of cancer is often caused by the emotion of despair. . .cancer patients are closing their eyes and *visualizing* their white blood cells inside their bodies waging victorious battles against their cancer cells—and their cancer gradually disappear. . . physicians are amazed at the powerful effect of "placebos" (sugar pills with no medical value whatsoever) given to patients deluded into thinking that they are taking real medicines, and resulting in miraculous cures. . .scientists in the USSR are diagnosing patients with high frequency radiation that photographs different-colored "auras" around the body, auras that change in color with the change of *emotions*.

More than ever before, both doctors and patients are becoming aware of the fact that many, if not most, of our diseases are actually psychosomatic*, and that illness is inseparably linked to the mind.

* *Psyche* (mind) affecting *soma* (body).

1

PSYCHOSOMATIC ILLNESS

Germs and viruses exist around us and within us all the time, and usually they do us no harm. Our immune system, the body's defenses–like the white blood cells that attack and devour harmful "invaders"–normally protect us from all infections, from common colds to major diseases. But when we are beset with negative emotions such as grief, despondency or anxiety, our immune system is weakened. Then the harmful bacteria get a chance to proliferate in our bodies–and we succumb to disease.

The link between negative emotions and the onset of disease has been confirmed again and again in recent years. Grief often precedes disease: in one study, 28 of 32 multiple sclerosis patients questioned experienced tragic or stressful life situations just before the onset of their disease, and this severe psychological stress was shown to have produced *marked abnormality in their bodies' immune systems.* [2] Doctors at Johns Hopkins Medical School found that extremely moody and emotional people are more likely to develop serious illness such as cancer, high blood pressure and heart disease, and die young*. And it is now commonly accepted by heart specialists that the "Type A" personality–competitive, hurried, impatient, and easily aggravated–is more prone to heart disease and heart attack.

Disturbing emotions such as sorrow, hatred, or envy, are like vibrational shock waves that affect the entire nervous system. For instance, the shock created by the sudden news of the death of a loved one may increase the blood pressure and place a tremendous strain on the heart. Nervous disorders and heart attack may result;

---

* Of two groups of people studied over a 30-year period, one emotionally balanced and the other emotionally imbalanced, 77% of the emotional group suffered major diseases, and only 25% of the emotionally balanced group.[3]

and in extreme sorrow or fear, even death may occur. It has been estimated that more than half the people seeking the service of doctors are actually suffering from emotionally-caused sicknesses: Emotional stresses–worry, fear, frustration, insecurity–are now known to be responsible for such diverse complaints as canker sores, peptic ulcers, heart attack, pneumonia, appendicitis, diabetes, asthma, schizophrenia and even cancer.

CANCER AND EMOTIONS

Cancer has been traditionally viewed as a strong and powerful invader that strikes the body from outside–a terrifying disease synonymous with death. But recent research has shown that cancer cells are not at all strong and powerful, but *weak* and *confused*. In fact, everyone has cancer once or twice in a lifetime; in a healthy individual the immune system will recognize these abnormal cells early in their development and destroy them; but when the immune system becomes weak, the mass of confused cells continues to grow. Cancer, then, is not an attack from without but a breakdown within. And what is the cause of this internal breakdown?– *negative emotions*, the scientists say, created by severe emotional stresses.

Psychological profiles of cancer patients have been established by many researchers, some of whom were even able to predict the incidence of cancer with amazing accuracy on the basis of these profiles. The following is the basic life pattern of many cancer patients, as confirmed by numerous studies: feelings of isolation, neglect, and despair during youth; a deep relationship with a person, or great satisfaction with a particular role (such as a job) in early adulthood, which becomes the center of the individual's life; loss of the relationship or role (through job loss, or the death or desertion of a loved one), resulting in feelings of despair, helplessness or hopelessness, which generally occur 6 to 18 months before the onset of the cancer; and finally the internalizing of the despair and the inability to express openly to others feelings of hurt, anger or hostility.[4]

These bottled-up negative emotions of despair and hopeless--ness create hormone imbalances that result in the increased production of abnormal cells, and weaken the body's immune system that should ordinarily destroy them. In fact, the difference between cancer cells and ordinary cells is that whereas the high voltage of ordinary cells blocks their abnormal division, cancer cells have an abnormally *low* voltage –they are permanently depolarized, so they easily proliferate.[5] This lowered energy level of the cancer cells is the direct physical manifestation of the patient's emotional "low", the sinking feelings of despair.

Glands and Emotions

We all feel emotions in our body; when we feel sad, we say, "I have a lump in my throat!"...when we feel fear, we say "I have butterflies in my stomach!" Anger: "My blood is boiling!" Disappointment: "My heart sank."[6]

Dr. Harold Streitfeld

This subtle interdependence of the mind and body is mediated by the *endocrine glands*, which conduct the complex symphony of the body by secreting chemical hormones into the bloodstream. These hormones have a profound effect not only on all the body's functions like growth, digestion, energy levels, heat, sexuality, etc., but on the mind as well.

In an experiment conducted in Sweden, the hormone content of a group of volunteers' urine was analyzed, and then they gathered to watch a movie. The film was a routine travelogue, and produced little emotional response in the audience. Urine samples collected after the film showed no important change in chemical content. The next day they watched a horror film, then a comedy, and later a war tragedy. The analysis of urine samples taken after these films disclosed marked alterations in the audience's production of hormones. The powerful emotions evoked by those films—fear, joy, sorrow—were accompanied by distinct glandular changes.[7]

5

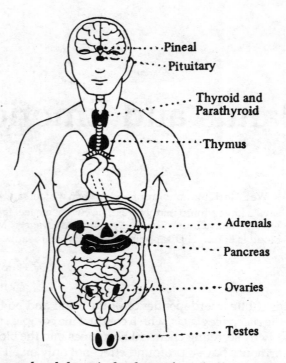

Pineal

Pituitary

Thyroid and
Parathyroid

Thymus

Adrenals

Pancreas

Ovaries

Testes

Hormone levels have indeed a profound effect on mood, temperament, and mental efficiency. Over or under-secretion of various glands can cause emotional and mental disturbances, which destroy health and peace of mind. Over-secretion of the hormone thyroxin from the thyroid gland, for instance, makes a perfectly normal person nervous and irritable. Women show marked optimism and enhanced self-confidence at the time of ovulation, when their estrogen and progesterone hormonal levels are high: but the same women become extremely anxious or hostile when their hormone levels hit bottom during their premenstrual and menstrual periods. One study revealed that *about half* of the psychiatric hospitalizations of women and criminal acts committed by women take place during these hormonal lows, and about 57% of attempted female suicides. Males are also subject to emotional ups and downs, determined by hormonal cycles similar to women's monthly menstrual rhythm.[5]

Thus there is a dynamic interaction between emotions, hormones and disease*–between body and mind.

YOGA A'SANAS

This interrelation was perceived long ago by yogis who developed a system of exercises to place specific pressure on the various endocrine glands. Thousands of years ago, deep in the ancient

* The tiny structure that links them all together may perhaps be the hypothalamus in the brain. The hypothalamus is part of the limbic brain, which *generates emotions;* it is also closely related to the *pituitary gland* which is one of the most important glands of the body; and it is also involved in the body's *immune system* and defense against disease (when animals are stimulated in the hypothalamic region their ability to make antibodies to fight disease markedly increases).

7

jungles of India and China, there lived yogis who had dedicated themselves to the mastery of their bodies and minds. In that peaceful environment, they used to carefully observe the animals that shared their solitude–how they moved, how they rested, how they instinctively cured themselves when sick. As they experimented with the different postures of the animals on their own bodies, they felt the subtle effects of these movements on their own organs and glands. Over thousands of years of experimentation, these animal postures which the yogis invented were refined into a scientific system of thousands of exercises called " àsanas", many of which were named after the animals which inspired them–cobra, hare, lion, flying bird, tortoise, monkey, peacock, etc.

A'sana literally means "posture comfortably held." The subtle pressure of the asana posture, held motionlessly for a certain length of time, restores the proper secretion of hormones, resulting in emotional balance and thus physical and mental health. Let us examine the functions of the endocrine glands in detail, and the effect of various a'sanas on these glands.

PINEAL GLANDS

The most mysterious gland in the human body is the pineal gland, located directly in the center of the brain. The ancient

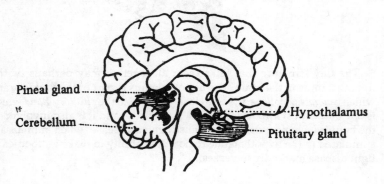

Pineal gland
Cerebellum
Hypothalamus
Pituitary gland

8

philosophers realized the tremendous importance of this tiny, mushroom-shaped gland, and called it the "seat of the Soul" and the "controller of thought." For many years western scientists ignored the importance of the pineal gland, but recently there has been a great increase of interest in the activity of this little gland. It has been found that long ago, in the evolutionary past, some undeveloped creatures such as lizards actually had a third eye in the top of their heads which was very sensitive to light and regulated the natural cyclical rhythms of their bodies. Gradually, over millions of years of evolution, this "eye" descended into the brain, and the pineal gland in human beings is the vestige of that primordial "third eye."

For centuries yogis have taught that the "third eye of intuition" when properly developed or "opened" by yoga practice, will produce a blissful state of mind, and a subtle intuitive awareness. Recent research has confirmed this ancient concept of the yogis, for the pineal gland has been found to secrete hormones such as seratonin and melatonin, which affect not only many of the organs of the body (by directly or indirectly activating all the glands below) but the state of the *mind* as well.

Because of the pineal gland's extreme sensitivity to light, during the darkness of night the amount of melatonin secreted by the pineal gland is very high and the amount of seratonin is very low. This produces a very relaxed state of body and mind, so the person can easily fall asleep. During the daylight, just the opposite occurs: the amount of melatonin decreases and the amount of seratonin increases, which produces a more restless state of activity.*

When the production of seratonin is gradually completely suspended, a person experiences a more and more peaceful state of being until he or she enters a state of higher awareness, and may experience feelings of intense inner happiness and a sense of oneness with all creation.

Throughout the centuries yogis have developed many physical and mental exercises designed specifically to directly affect the pineal gland and thus attain subtler mental awareness—such as certain meditation techniques, or asanas like the Hare Pose (*Shasháungásana*). In the Hare Pose the crown of the head is repeatedly pressed against the ground, which massages the pineal gland in the brain. In this way, the production of melatonin is increased and seratonin gradually decreased; thus the posture develops

---

* It is interesting that the color green decreases the amount of seratonim produced by the pineal gland. That is probably why we associate the color green with a more relaxed mood.

patience and tranquility of mind, and makes it easier to attain intuitional insight.

PITUITARY GLAND

The pituitary has been called the "master gland" by medical science; however, in reality it functions as a relay station for impulses arising in the hypothalamus in the brain, which coordinates the nervous system with the glandular system. The pituitary gland then relays the messages from the hypothalamus to all the endocrine glands of the body. The pituitary hormones excite the movement of the bowels, keep the blood vessels toned up, and stimulate the kidneys to do their work. They also help to regulate the body's temperature and control growth and development; improper secretion of the pituitary gland results in the abnormal growth of extremely obese people, giants and midgets.

11

THYROID AND PARATHYROID GLANDS

The thyroid gland in the neck (with its lobes on either side of the larynx) controls the metabolic rate of the body, the speed at which the chemical processes of the body occur. Like a thermostat, it regulates the level of body heat and energy produced. Among other things, it regulates growth, repair and waste processes. The hormonal secretions from the parathyroid glands regulate calcium and phosphorus metabolism.

Any imbalance in the thyroid gland has serious consequences. Even a slight over-secretion of the thyroid hormone will result in intense irritability, while marked over-secretion ("hyperthyroidism") will cause extreme nervousness, heart palpitation or sleeplessness, gastro-intestinal disturbances, tremours and rapid pulse, excessive perspiration, and loss of weight. Undersecretion, on the other hand, will create a feeling of fatigue and lethargy: and marked undersecretion (hypothyroidism) will cause sluggish metabolism, mental dullness, slow pulse, low temperature, blunted appetite, drawling speech and obesity.

It is clear then, that the balanced secretion of the thyroid hormone is essential for the health of the body and mind, and for this the yogis developed the Shoulderstand and Fish postures. In the Shoulderstand (*Sarvāungāsana*, page 66) the thyroid gland is squeezed by the pressure of the chin against the chest, and in the Fish Pose (page 67), which is alternated with the Shoulderstand three times, it is stretched. So the combination of these two poses effectively massages the thyroid gland and increases the blood flow to it, balancing its secretions and improving its overall function—and thus enhancing the health of body and mind.

THE THYMUS GLAND

The thymus gland, located behind the breastbone, is very large during childhood but at puberty begins to shrivel up to one-fourth of its original size. It is generally agreed that the thymus exerts a primary role in regulating the immunal defenses of the body against disease, but the details of this mechanism—and other functions of the thymus—are not yet known.

ADRENAL GLANDS

The adrenal glands, located just on top of the kidneys, help govern sudden bursts of energy and heat, and stimulate the twin responses of staying to fight or running away (the "fight or flight" response). In a crisis, when everything depends on muscular exertion, the brain sends a nervous message to these glands, which promptly pour their secretions into the bloodstream. The secretion, ADRENALIN, speeds up the heart and dilates the blood vessels to the muscles, and stimulates the sweat glands so that the body may be cooled. It slows down the movements of the digestive organs and contracts their blood-vessels; it makes the liver shed its stored sugar so that the muscles may have a copious supply of fuel; it stands the hair on end, dilates the pupils and widens the eyes, so that the individual may be terrifying to look upon. It is a chemical S.O.S.

A person whose adrenal glands are not able to secrete sufficient adrenalin, will not be able to respond properly in a crisis. On the other hand, one whose glands oversecrete or secrete inappropriately, will be in a continuous state of nervous tension.

PANCREAS

The pancreas lies just below the stomach and secretes digestive enzymes into the small intestine, such as INSULIN, a hormone which lowers the amount of energy-giving glucose in the blood. Defects in the pancreas cause diabetes.

GONADS

The gonads (ovaries and testes) primarily govern the sexual function. In the female, the ovaries are located in the abdominal area, and in the male the testes are located in the scrotum, the bag hanging below the penis. These glands not only produce sperm and egg cells, but also secrete ANDROGENS (male sex hormones) and ESTROGENS (female sex hormones). These sex hormones regulate the physical development of the body and the sexual patterns of the individual.

For example, androgens increase the muscular mass of the body and seem to induce aggressive behavior; estrogens increase fatty padding and may promote passive behavior. Everyone's body produces *both* androgens and estrogens; it is the proper proportion of these hormones which balances the personality.

EFFECT OF ASANAS

Thus the entire human organism—every organ, tissue and cell is affected by the hormones, and the proper growth and functioning of the various parts of the body is possible only when there is a *balanced secretion* of all these hormones; any imbalance results in disease.

Asanas balance the hormonal secretions from the various glands: the twisting and bending positions of the asanas, held for a

14

specific period of time, place continued and specific pressure on the glands, thus stimulating them in various ways and regulating their secretions, and controlling the emotions as well. As glandular defects are cured, the mind is relieved of one upsetting emotional tendency after another, and perfect mental composure is ultimately attained.

Different asanas are prescribed to students free of charge by trained teachers of Ananda Marga to strengthen or regulate the secretion of various glands; for example, the Bow Pose (*Dhanurásana*, page 70) and the Wheel Pose (*Cakrásana*, page 69) affect the adrenal glands, etc. By the regular practice of asanas, many common ailments can be alleviated, and the body and mind's harmony restored.

Physiological Benefits of A'sanas

The first signs of practicing yoga are lightness,
health, absence of desire, a good complexion, a beautiful
voice, and an agreeable odor of the body. . .

Svetasvatara Upanisad

A'sanas affect every aspect of the human physique; they not
only balance the glandular secretions, but they also relax and tone
up the muscles and the nervous system, stimulate circulation,
stretch stiff ligaments and tendons, limber joints, massage the
internal organs, and calm and concentrate the mind. During these
smooth motions the body remains in a state of relaxed efficiency,
and the deep breathing which naturally accompanies these postures carries a great deal of oxygen to be absorbed in the bloodstream. During a'sana practice, energy is accumulated rather than
spent.

Gradually, as the body becomes more accustomed to these
limbering, relaxing exercises, all physical activity becomes an
extension of a'sanas, done at moderate speed with smooth flowing
motions, deep breathing to afford the body plenty of oxygen and a
calm and controlled mind, alert and responsive to the needs of any
situation.

Better keep yourself clean and bright; you are the
window through which you must see the world.

George Bernard Shaw

16

The Muscles

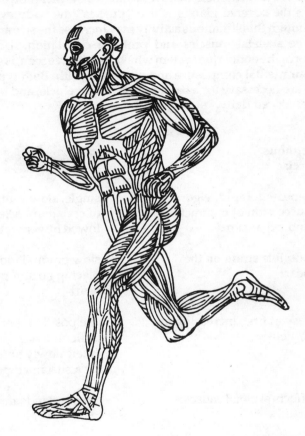

    In the very name "a'sana" – "posture comfortably held" – lies the key to the differences between yogic exercises and other systems of physical exercise. Calisthenics and gymnastics tend to develop the muscles by making them work: they stress movement, and commonly alternate violent movements of expansion and contraction, generally in fairly quick succession. These rapidly repeated exercises increase in difficulty and are often competitive in nature; the excitement in turn stimulates the secretion of adrenalin from the adrenal glands which "pushes" the body even harder. Although this strenuous activity may increase the size and strength of the skeletal muscles and promote circulation, it completely ignores the endocrine system which, as we have seen, is so essential to our mental composure and physical health. Both types of exercise are necessary for a balanced physical vehicle, and both should be practiced daily.

Strenuous Exercise	A'sanas
* repeated, rapid, vigorous succession of contractions and expansions	* single, slow contraction of certain muscles followed by general relaxation
* possible strain on the heart	* slow gradual movements placing no strain on the heart
* easy at first, increasing in difficulty	* one position, perhaps difficult to take up, but taken slowly and held for a sustained period
* effects skeletal muscles mainly	* effects glands mainly
* competitive (in group or with oneself)	* solitary, emphasis on tranquility and poise
* effect mainly physical	* effect mainly mental

NO LACTIC ACID FATIGUE

When muscles contract, the stored sugar in the body breaks down to lactic acid and additional energy is released. Much of the lactic acid thus produced, however, must be further converted into water and carbon dioxide (H_2O and CO_2), by combining with oxygen. In strenuous exercise, the lungs breathe faster and faster in order to get sufficient oxygen to meet these muscular demands. But if the exercise is very strenuous, even rapid and deep breathing is unable to supply the body's need for oxygen to oxidize and convert this lactic acid into water and carbon dioxide. As a result, an excess of lactic acid accumulates in the muscles and they become fatigued and unable to contract, or painfully cramped.

On the other hand, in moderate exercises such as a'sanas, the oxygen supply can keep pace with the oxygen used, so no excess lactic acid accumulates, and no fatigue results. Thus the slow gradual movements of asanas put no unnecessary strain on the heart, muscles or nervous system.

INCREASED CIRCULATION

Both a'sanas and strenuous exercises contract the skeletal muscles, which then squeeze down on the veins more vigorously and help them to pump blood back to the heart more quickly. This greater flow of blood to the heart due to muscular contraction fills the heart more than usual, resulting in a more forceful contraction of the heart in its beat, and more blood is pumped out (this is known as Starling's Law of the Heart). The faster heart rate and stronger contraction of the cardiac muscle stimulates faster and deeper breathing and more thorough ventilation of the lungs. The end result is a greater flow of blood, carrying an increased supply of oxygen and fuel to the cells. These increased supplies are largely consumed during violent exercise, whereas during the moderate exercise of asanas there is only a moderate energy demand; as a

19

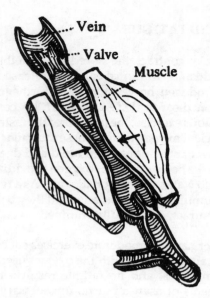

....Vein

··· Valve

Muscle

result the body receives an energy bonus—energy is accumulated rather than spent.*

EXERCISE OF LITTLE-USED MUSCLES

Some muscles of the body are almost never used, even in systematic strenuous exercises. Asanas are designed to exercise *all* the muscles of a given part of the body. In this way, some muscles usually tending to atrophy because of poor use, such as certain muscles of the ribs and stomach, are restored to good operation.

---

*   Indeed, a recent study at Emory University in the USA concluded that asanas have exactly the *same* beneficial effects on the heart, lungs and circulatory system as vigorous gymnastics and calisthenics, without lactic acid accumulation in the muscles, exhaustion or muscle pain.

RELAXED MUSCULAR TONE

In the normal person, even during sleep or rest, the muscles are rarely in a state of complete rest. Within them there always persists a certain degree of tension, called *basal tension* or *muscular tone*, which is necessary to maintain the normal configuration and posture of our bodies. However, the maintenance of this muscular tone also uses up energy even when our bodies are not moving.

A'sanas, as opposed to vigorous exercises, involve a single slow contraction of certain muscles, sustained for a specific period of time, followed by general relaxation. "After an a'sana position has been maintained long enough, a group of muscles are 'depolarized', that is, made completely inert. In other words, through the a'sanas it is possible to obtain, in an entirely natural way, what medicine has not yet been able to achieve: to induce *a selective muscular relaxation*, limited to particular groups of muscles, without involvement of the entire somatic muscular system (as occurs following drug injections)."[9] The perfect, selective relaxation induced by the a'sanas involves a tremendous saving of energy, which can then be redirected inward, for the elevation of the mind to higher states of consciousness.

The Spine

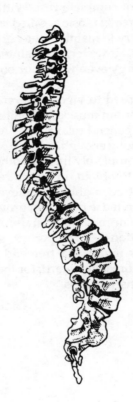

The body's axis, the spine, is composed of many individual vertebrae separated by cushions, or discs. This column supports the weight of the body, enabling it to move in many directions: standing, bending, swaying, twisting. Each individual vertebrae has a hole in it, through which runs the spinal cord, an extension of the brain matter into the body. The spinal cord has nerves running in and out of it between every two vertebrae, which control the sensory and motor functions of the whole body.*

The human body can assume many different positions, but three of them are basic: upright, sitting, and lying down. In each of these positions, the vertebral column plays an essential role in maintaining the body's equilibrium. Physics teaches us that to maintain the body's equilibrium, the axis of gravity should fall between the feet when they are spread apart. If an individual can maintain this position of natural physical equilibrium, the strain on his or her vertebral muscles is minimum, and all the weight of the body is harmoniously distributed along the 32 vertebrae of the spinal column.

But when an individual bends the vertebral column, he or she moves the body's center of gravity forward, and it no longer lies between the tips of the feet but is situated farther forward. As a result, the static equilibrium of the body is disturbed, and a mending job must begin to maintain the balance. This adjustment is carried out by the paravertebral muscles surrounding the spine, which are then strained to a point where the well-known backache appears. Some people maintain that "with the inevitable backache,

* Except the head and some special organ functions governed by the vagus nerve.

human beings pay for the privilege of being the only creature on earth made to live in an upright position." This is entirely incorrect. On the contrary, it may be said that with their backaches, human beings pay for their refusal to live in a proper upright position, as they were intended to by Mother Nature, choosing instead to live and walk like apes, with their posture totally projected forward.[10]

It might seem that bed rest should, at least in part, remove the fatigue of the back muscles. But when one observes the way people usually rest and sleep, literally spread all over the bed, or cuddled up like a foetus in the mother's womb, one can easily understand why upon awakening, the back will be just as painful as before, if not worse. Thus in order to obtain true rest from sleep and relaxation, one should lie in a supine position, or sleep on the right side, with the back straight. This later position not only completely relaxes the muscles and nervous system, but also has a subtle beneficial effect on the body's vital energies (see page 61), that keeps the mind tranquil and calm during sleep and less prone to disturbing dreams.

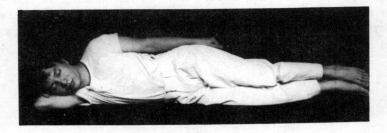

The correct position of the vertebral column in all positions—upright, sitting, lying down—not only maintains the proper equilibrium of the body and rests the vertebral muscles, but is also essential for correct breathing—for the free expansion of the chest—and for the harmonious operation of the nervous system as well. When the nerves are pinched by the improper position of the spinal column, many painful conditions and diseases result.

An erect spine also has important psychological side effects. Physical and mental equilibrium are closely connected; it is difficult for a person who is physically imbalanced to maintain mental equipoise. Depressed people usually walk with bent shoulders and curved backs. As they stoop forward, their paravertebral muscles are chronically strained and aching. This chronic back pain in turn contributes to their mental depression, in a dangerous vicious cycle of psychosomatic illness.

As Dr. Steven Brena, a noted researcher on the medical benefits of yoga asanas, has said, "Take note of the statues of the Pharaohs and of the Egyptian priests. Observe the sculptures of the Assyrians, of the Babylonians, and the Greeks. Look at the attitude of the Hindu emperors and divinities. Notice their perfect erect position, their vertebral columns straight as a poker ... The ancients knew, better than we, the importance of correct vertebral position as the prime expression of human dignity.[11]

POSTURE AND LIGAMENTS

Small infants naturally move their spines in a variety of positions, but this flexibility is lost as the body grows. An average person of 30 years can no longer touch the floor with his or her fingertips when the knees are straight. Why?

The reason for this restriction of body movements is the progressive *shortening of ligaments and tendons*. Ligaments are bands or sheets of fibrous tissue, connecting two or more bones, cartilage, or other structures; tendons connect muscles to bones. As a person grows older, the backbone stiffens because the ligaments become tighter. And since ligamentous structures are continuous, if mobility is restricted in any area, the smooth flow of movement of the entire body is affected.

The cause of the shortening of the ligaments and tendons are those troublemakers, bad posture and poor balance. The spinal column has four curves, all of which lend resilience and spring to the vertebral column and are essential for walking and jumping. Improper posture may exaggerate these curves fo the vertebral column. For example, those who sit much of the time—students, office workers, artists, writers—thrust their heads and necks forward. This awkward posture shortens the ligaments and causes the spine to become rounded. These shortened, tightened ligaments and tendons compress and irritate nerves, causing headaches and severe pains in the neck and shoulders.

EFFECT OF A´SANAS

Each a´sana pose exercises the spine, exposing it to stretching, tensions and twistings of various degrees. All this prevents and corrects wrong positions of the spine in all positions: upright, sitting and lying down. If you observe a sincere yoga practitioner, you will at once notice the correct, agile and elegant way which he or she sits, stands and moves.

(Dear Reader, how are you sitting right now?)

Yogis, who long ago realized the importance of the perfect health of the spinal column for human life designed many asanas especially to maintain the proper curvature of the spine, such as the Fish, the Cobra, and the Spinal Twist (pages 67, 76 and 68). The Full-Head-to-Knee Pose (page 74) stretches the spine to its maximum length, *20% over the normal length of the spine in sitting.*

These positions also stretch the ligaments and tendons which wrap the spine, thus relieving the painful compression of the nerves. And by strengthening the muscles of the spine, they maintain its proper curvature. In this way, asanas restore the childlike flexibility of the spinal column, and prevent the painful stiffening of the body as it ages.

The Joints

All of the bones in the human body are connected with one another through the articulations, or joints, the majority of which work like ball joints. The articulations suffer enormous wear and tear because of the constant and dual nature of the work they must perform: for, besides working as mechanical joints between two adjoining bones, some articulations are constantly pressed by body weight. Think of the amount of weight the joints of the lower limbs

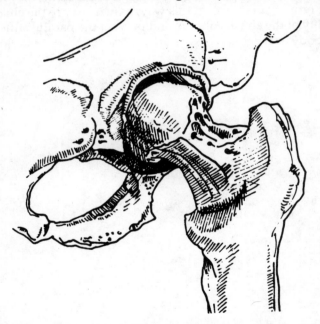

must support and move during an obese person's lifetime! The situation becomes still worse when imbalanced and improper living further damages the joints: insufficient physical exercise and digestive toxins,* especially from the meats, tend to "rust" the articulations before their time and make even a young person look and feel prematurely old.

This "rusting" of the joints is called *osteoarthritis* and results in the progressive destruction of the soft cartilage tissue which covers the ends of the bones. When this cartilage gradually disintegrates, the two extremities of the bones, no longer protected by the soft tissue, gradually join together, and the whole joint disappears. If the arthritis, as frequently happens, destroys the knee or hip joint, one day the individual finds himself or herself in a wheelchair, or confined to the "dreadful immobility" of a bed.[12]

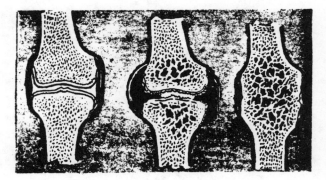

Yoga a'sanas lubricate and exercise the joints, breaking up and dissolving the "rust" and restoring their free and natural movements.** New students of yoga soon start to feel their joints rapidly becoming more and more agile with repeated practice of the a'sanas, until their bodies become, once again, as flexible and agile as a child's.

* Such as calcium and uric acid deposits.
** Beginning practitioners may actually hear cracking sounds performing the postures, which may be the calcium deposits in the joints breaking up (or it may also be the ligaments passing over the bones.)

The Circulation

One of the major killers in many countries of the world is *arteriosclerosis,* or hardening of the arteries. In this dangerous condition, the inner walls of the arteries become coated with a layer of bright-yellow fats, especially cholesterol. These fatty deposits may

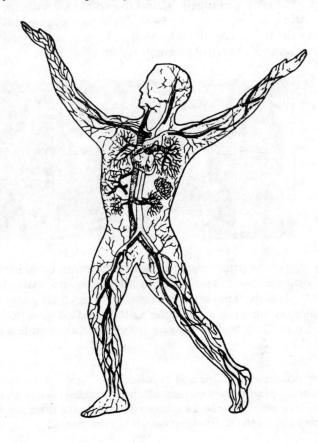

then calsify, turning the arteries into brittle pipes. These clogged and often stiff arteries allow less and less blood to flow through; this in turn places a tremendous burden on the heart, which then has to pump harder and harder to send the blood through the congested vessels. As a result, high blood pressure and heart attack occur; or the vessels may rupture, causing hemorrhage, or eventually clog up completely, causing the death of the tissues the arteries would normally supply. When this occurs in the brain it is called a "stroke"; if it occurs in the arteries of the heart, it results in heart attack. Autopsies performed on young soldiers killed in the Korean War showed that 25% of them had already begun to exhibit signs of the disease.

The twisting and stretching postures of a'sanas stretch the blood vessels, thus increasing their elasticity, and preventing their stiffening and obstruction by harmful toxins. Elastic arteries maintain proper pressure in between the beats of the heart, and thus keep the blood flowing steadily, not in spurts. This steady flow of blood provides an even supply to all parts of the body; the stimulated circulation bathes the tissues with the proper nutrients and oxygen and removes waste toxins, thus maintaining the body's tissues in perfect working order.

CURING VARICOSE VEINS

The veins return the blood to the heart by means of valves. If these valves in the lower extremities start to wear out and malfunction, then the veins swell, producing the unsightly and painful condition of varicose veins in the legs. Certain reverse yoga postures such as Shoulderstand, Plough, etc. have a special beneficial effect on the valves in the veins; for during these a'sanas the blood from the extremities flows back to the heart without effort. This reduces the usual pressures on the valves and gives them a rest they would not normally obtain when the body is upright. And only during these reverse postures can all the tiny blood vessels in the lower extremities, the capillaries, have a chance to drain completely, which thoroughly cleanses the tissues. As a result of the repeated practice of these postures, the clogged veins are cleared, and the painful swelling of varicose veins may be completely removed.

Internal Organs

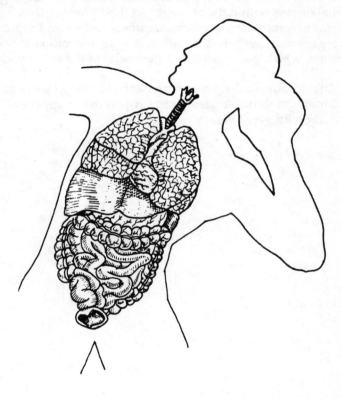

Asanas tone up the entire system. They give internal massage, pressure and stretch the organs such as the stomach and the liver, and improve the circulation of blood to these organs. This keeps all the organs in healthy operating condition, easily able to respond quickly and accurately to the "orders" coming from the various glands.

For example, the Shoulderstand Pose relieves tension on the lower abdominal muscles and organs, while simultaneously allowing the clogged pelvic and leg veins to drain down instead of up. Other asanas strengthen the abdominal walls, thus keeping the internal organs within the abdomen in their proper place. In this way, the sagging of the stomach, intestines, kidney and reproductive organs may easily be prevented. Asanas also promote proper digestion, which is so essential to the health of the entire body.

In addition, in deep diaphragmatic breathing (see page 53), the diaphragm muscle massages the organs in the upper abdominal cavity with every breath.

Prána: The Life Force

Throughout the universe, the yogis say, pulsates a single, universal energy, the origin and sum of all forces – gravitational, electric, magnetic, and human vital energy as well. The yogis call this universal energy *prána;** The Chinese call it *chi* and the Japanese, *ki.* This fundamental energy pervades and controls every living organism; we are all surrounded by an invisible "life field", in constant flow and rhythmic pulsation, that organizes our vital functions and gradually disappears at death. But we are so conditioned to look *out* of our bodies that we have become unaware of this subtle inner force, far subtler than electromagnetic energy; we think of ourselves only as gross physical bodies made of flesh and do not realize that we are "diaphanous webs" of pulsating energy fields in continual flux and interaction with the energy fields around us, as far away as the distant stars.

For centuries, yogis and psychicly developed people have maintained that the human body is surrounded by an envelope of energy that radiates different colors depending on the individual's state' but materialistic scientists scorned this idea as mere "foolishness". Recently a remarkable technique was developed in the Soviet Union to actually *photograph* this "energy body" and thus to confirm its existence once and for all.

---

* This all-pervasive vital energy has been discovered and rediscovered throughout western history as well, and has been given many names from "odic force" to "X force," from "orgone energy" to "etheric force."

This technique, called *Kirlian photography* after its inventor, places the object to be photographed inside a field of high frequency electrical currents.* One scientist who viewed a Kirlian photograph of his own hands exclaimed, "An unseen world opened up before my eyes! Whole luminescent labyrinths, flashing, twinkling, flaring. Some of the sparks were motionless, constantly glittering; others came and went like wandering stars. Over these fantastic galaxies of ghostly lights there were bright multicolored flares of blue, orange and blazing violet, fiery flashes ..."[13]

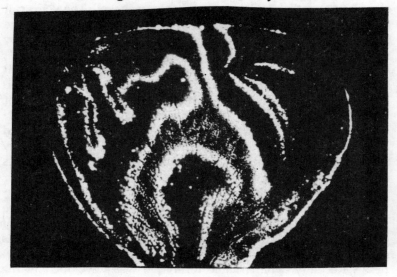

Kirlian photograph of a leaf

* A high-frequency spark generator or oscillator generates 75,000 to 200,000 electrical oscillations per second, which creates a powerful field between two clamps. Objects, along with photographic paper, are then placed between these two clamps, and the complex patterns of colors are radiated directly onto the photographic paper, even without the use of a camera. The scientist Kirlian also developed special techniques to observe the changing energy patterns in motion.

As a result of much experimentation with Kirlian photography, scientist have found that this "energy body" or "bioplasma" as the Soviets call it, manifests changes in an organism long before they appear on the gross physical level: a fatal plant disease was detected in a plant's energy aura many days before it appeared in the physical body of the leaf. The Soviets are now using Kirlian photography to detect the early onset of disease, especially cancer, in the "bioplasma" long before it would ordinarily be discovered in the physical body. [14]

This force field seems to be the organizing pattern which guides the growth of the physical body, for it determines the physical form the growing tissue will take: if a bit of protoplasm from the arm location of a developing embryo is placed in the leg position of that embryo, it will become a *leg*. And the energy body may persist even after the physical counterpart has been removed: Kirlian photographs taken of a leaf with one-third of it cut away were the *same* as photographs of the complete leaf!* Scientists suspect that it is this energy body that amputees feel when they swear they can still feel their missing leg, or arm.

This also seems to be the energy psychic healers radiate during their miraculous cures. Kirlian photography during psychic healing revealed a general decreasing of the overall brightness of the healer's hand, and a narrow focused channel of intense, laser-like brilliance, emanating from the center. It is this powerful flow of *prána* radiating from the bioplasmic energy body of the healer to the energy body of the sick patient that balances and revitalizes it, and eventually heals it. This radiant energy, indeed, can recharge everything around it: one psychic healer held water in a sealed flask

* However if more han one-third of the leaf is cut away, the structural solidarity of the leaf is lost and as it dies, the whole energy body gradually vanishes.

which was later poured over barley seeds. Those seeds quickly *outgrew* all the others which had not been watered by the irradiated water. (Conversely, when depressed or mentally sick patients held the water, the seeds' growth was severely retarded. A sick person can kill a yeast culture merely by holding it in his or her hand!) [15]

The color and pattern of this vital energy immediately changes with the change in emotional states: photographs of the hand of a calm, relaxed person show small amounts of energy issuing from the fingertips, whereas the land of a nervous or angry person shows great wide streams of vital energy chaotically escaping.

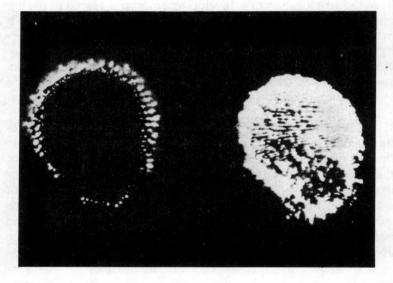

Kirlian photographs of the thumb of a person taken when relaxed and calm (left) and when angry (right). A tranquil individual radiates a bluish-white glow; when upset, the color changes to bright red.

From these Kirlian photographs, scientists have learned that our energy body is immediately affected by everything in its surroundings. It detects fear, aggression, panic, or friendliness in the people around it. It responds to force fields produced by machines, by the sun, moon and planets, by thunderstorms, noise and wind; it resonates to changes in the seasons and ocean tides, and especially to electromagnetic disturbances on the sun ("sunspots").* What is beginning to emerge is

> ... a new picture of the human being, not an alien-
> ated creature, but a pulsating field, dynamically in
> teracting with all other fields, like a note resonating
> with all the other notes swirling in a symphony. It
> is a new view of the human being linked to the cos-
> mos, aware of and reacting—by means of his or her "bi-
> oplasmic energy body"—to changes in the sun and plan-
> ets, environment, weather and machines, as well as to
> the illnesses, moods and thoughts of others; a view of
> humanity as an enmeshed, integral part of life on earth
> and in the universe. [16]

THE OCEAN OF PRÁNA

Long ago, yogis, with their deep intuitional insight, realized that all entities exist within this vast ocean of cosmic

* This explains the fact that psychic powers such as psychokinesis and ESP diminish in stormy weather and are heightened during sunspots and magnetic disturbances. Indeed, this energy body seems to be greatly affected by atmospheric changes, especially the ionization (electrically charged particles) of the air. It is revitalized by negative ions (negatively charged particles), which proliferate in mountain heights and near rushing water such as waterfalls; and it is fatigued and weakened by positive ions, such as those created by pollution, air conditioning, or by the warm, dry desert winds that sweep periodically through many regions of the world.

prāná, whose waves of energy are constantly arising and dissolving with infinite variety. They learned how to harness and control that vast power of the cosmic energy within them, and this control over their prana not only unfolded their artistic and intellectual capabilities but gave them tremendous psychic powers as well.

Suppose, for instance, a person understood *prāná* perfectly and could control it, what power on earth would not be his or hers? He or she would be able to move the sun and stars out of their places, to control everything in the universe from the atoms to the biggest suns. The great world-movers, the prophets and heroes, had the most wonderful control over their *prāná*, which gave them tremendous will-power. They were able to bring their *prāná* to a high state of vibration, so that they drew thousands to them and influenced half the world. [17]

THE CAKRAS

These ancient sages not only detected this "bioplasmic energy" within them but also mapped out the exact flow of its current in the body* and described the seven energy centers or *cakras* (pronounced "chakras") which control these fluctuating force fields. Recently science has finally detected these *cakras* as well: sensitive instruments have measured

---

* These subtle energy currents are called *nādiis* and correspond to the Chinese description of the flow of *chi* throughout the body. The Chinese science of acupuncture was developed to correct imbalanced energy flows in these subtle currents, thereby curing disease. Interestingly, Kirlian photographs of flares of energy leaving the body at various locations correspond *exactly* to the acupuncture points!

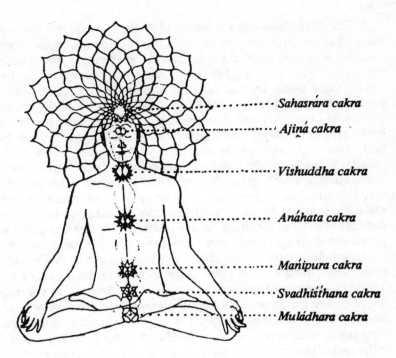

- Sahasrára cakra
- Ajiná cakra
- Vishuddha cakra
- Anáhata cakra
- Manipura cakra
- Svadhisthana cakra
- Muládhara cakra

energy emanations (*beyond* frequencies which are known to come from biochemical, anatomical systems) surging from the surface of the body *at the exact location of the cakras.* [18]

These *cakras* are more subtle than the physical nervous system and cannot be seen by the naked eye; they can be perceived only when one develops the intuitional "inner sight" to experience them from within. Each *cakra* controls a particular area and component factor of the body, and is related to certain endocrine glands. For the *cakras* control the operation of the body and mind by means of the glands, by stimulating the glands to produce their various hormones. Just as the higher glands control the lower ones, so the higher *cakras* control the lower ones also.

41

The *Múládhara cakra* (located near the base of the body at the end of the spinal cord) controls the solid factor in the body and is directly related to the gonads and the excretory functions of the anus. The next higher (and more subtle) *cakra* is the *Svádhisthána cakra*, located slightly higher on the spine, which controls the liquid factor of the body and is related to the sexual glands and the body's sexual function. The *Manipura cakra* at the navel area controls the luminous factor (heat and energy) of the body and digestion, and is related to the pancreas and adrenal glands. The fourth *cakra*, the *Anáhata cakra*, located in the center of the chest, controls the aerial factor and is related to the respiratory and circulatory functions of the body. The fifth cakra, *Vishuddha cakra* (located in the throat), controls the ethereal factor, the subtlest of the five elements, and is related to the thyroid and and parathyroid glands; it is responsible for speech. This *cakra* controls all those below it; thus it coordinates all the energies of the physical body. The "third eye" of *Ájiná cakra*, located in the center of the brain, is sometimes called the "seat of the mind." It controls the pituitary gland and the hypothalamus, and the mental functioning. The seventh and highest *cakra*, the *Sahasrára cakra* at the very center and top of the head, is related to the pineal gland and is the seat of pure consciousness in the individual. It controls all the *cakras* below it, and is thus the controlling center of the entire organism.

The physical, mental and spiritual health of the individual depends on the proper energy balance between these *cakras* and between all the endocrine glands to which they are related. Disease is caused by a weakness, an imbalance in the energy flow of one or more of the *cakras*. Yoga teachers are trained to "diagnose" which of the *cakras* has become weakened in the case of illness, and then to prescribe the a'sana which will stimulate and re-energize that energy center and balance the secretion of the various glands. If improper a'sanas are performed for a certain condition, the practitioner may not only be wasting his or her time, but also harming the body as well. Thus it is never advisable to practice asanaś simply from books, but only under the guidance of trained teachers.

> *At this stage of evolution, yoga practitioners really know they are immersed in the infinite Ocean of Cosmic Energy, themselves a part of the Universe. Not only do they perceive the prána in the air they breathe, but likewise they feel its presence in the vegetables, in the fruits, in the cereals they feed on; they smell it in the flowers, hear it in the sounds, see it in the lights and colours that make this earthly world of ours so beautiful to those who can see it correctly. In other words, the Yogi has inserted his or her own vital cycle into Nature's biological cycles and feels one with the whole creation. Carbon, oxygen, nitrogen, hydrogen and the other chemical elements of which our body is made up, are the same ones present in the sun, in the planets, in the stars. From this intuitive solidarity, the Yogi comes to love all of Creation, and starts to realize the Unity that lies behind the various phenomena.*
>
> Dr. Steven Brena

Prána and the Breath

One of the remarkable discoveries of Kirlian photography is that the colored energy aura becomes *much brighter* when the lungs are filled with pure oxygen–that *deep breathing seems to generate and replenish this práhic energy*. For thousands of years yogis have understood the crucial relationship of vital energy to breathing, for we absorb this life-giving *prána* not only through the food we eat but especially through the air we breathe.

> Every living being depends upon breathing, and cessation of breathing is cessation of life. From the first cry of the infant to the last gasp of a dying person, there is nothing but a series of breaths. We constantly drain our life force or pranic energy by our every thought, every act of will or motion of muscles. In consequence, constant replenishing is necessary, which is possible through breathing alone.[19]

Thus Yogis have always emphasized the importance of proper breathing, and they developed a series of specific exercises called *práháyama* (breath control) to maximize the amount of vital energy absorbed with every breath. In ordinary breathing we extract only very little prana from the atmosphere. But when we concentrate and consciously regulate our breathing, we are able to store up a great amount of *prána* in the various nerve centers or *cakras*. Those who practice systematic and deep breathing can feel the tremendous vitalizing effect of the absorption of *prána*, as every part of the body becomes filled with vital energy. Eventually the whole body comes under our control, and all diseases can be destroyed from the root. In addition, this powerful pranic vitality produces health and energy in those around us, because our *prána* is conveyed to other bodies like water flowing from a higher level to a lower one.

Proper control of breathing can alleviate many diseases of modern humanity–heart disease, high and low blood pressure, asthma, and tuberculosis, among others. An increasingly popular natural method of childbirth, the La Maze method, teaches pregnant women deep breathing exercises similar to yogic breathing, to relieve the pain of childbirth. Breath control dissolves emotional tensions and relaxes the mind, and increases will power, concentration and self-control. And, most importantly, it accelerates spiritual development, for it accumulates tremendous inner force which can then be used to elevate the mind and enable one to shape a consciousness of a high order.

BREATHING AND THE MIND

"Thought commences and corresponds with vibration. When a man entertains a long thought, he draws a long breath; when he thinks quickly, his breath vibrates with rapid alternation; when the tempest of anger shakes his mind, his breath is tumultuous; when his soul is deep and tranquil, so is his respiration. But let him make trial of the contrary: let him endeavor to think in long stretches, at the same time that he breathes in fits, and he will find that it is impossible."

Emmanuel Swendenborg

A harmonious mind, corresponds to slow, deep and regular respiration; a troubled mind speeds up the heart and breathing rhythm, which then becomes irregular and broken. All of us experience this occurrence whenever we pant or are short of breath because of some sudden emotion. Some people's breath becomes shallow and irregular even in very mildly tense situations, like waiting for an interview or writing a letter. Conversely, rapid breathing limits the mental faculties; after running track, a school-boy cannot immediately sit down and solve his math problems; he protests, "Wait till I catch my breath!"

According to Yogic science, this is due to the action of the *pránendriya,* a psychic force located at the *Anáhata* cakra (the heart *cakra*). The *pránendriya* is pulsative, flowing in repeated waves of expansion and contraction. The subtle energy currents of the body vibrate sympathetically with the *pránendriya* and flow in its pattern. When the *pránendriya* is in the state of expansion or speed the subtle energy currents are also in a state of activity; as a result it is more difficult for the nerves to carry sensations from the outside to the brain, and perception is impaired. When the *pránendriya* is paused, however, the flow of energy is calm and the mind is in a tranquil state of receptivity. In this state vibrations from outside are received and registered clearly in the mind like the reflections on a still, smooth pond.

The *pránendriya* is closely related to respiration. According to Yogic science, the act of respiration is actually four-fold: inhalation (*púraka*), an inhalatory pause (*kumbhaka*), expiration (*recaka*), and an expiratory pause (*sunyaka*). During inhalation and exhalation the *pránendriya* is in a state of speed and expansion; during the pause the *pránendriya* is in a state of contraction or rest.

When the breathing is fast and irregular, the *pránendriya* is in a state of activity and the pause periods are short; as a result perception is unclear and the mind is disturbed. When the breath-

46

ing is slow, deep and regular, however, the pause periods are longer, the *pránendriya* is calm, and the power of receptivity and concentration of the mind increases. In a deep concentrative state, the respiration becomes slower and slower.

Western medical science is beginning to realize the close relation between the rate of breathing and mental states. Experiments have shown that changes in the respiratory rate correspond not only to rhythmic changes in the heart rate, but to changes in the electric potentials on the surface of the brain, that occur in response to outside stimulation. In addition, scientists are discovering that breathing may have a profound relation to mental moods as well. In experiments performed on persons concentrating, one doctor found that the concentrative state, which is characterized by a significant decrease in the respiratory rate, produces a marked *increased in skin resistance* – a measure which correspondence to *a decrease of anxiety.*

Dr. Peter Steincrohn has found that many of his patients who suffer from severe attacks of anxiety are shallow, rapid breathers. Dr. Steincoln calls this "overbreathing"; "Many people who have anxiety suffer from overbreathing and don't even suspect it. They overbreathe unconsciously by taking rapid, shallow breaths when nervous, which only intensifies their nervousness. They sigh or yawn often. They complain, "I can't seem to take a good breath. It isn't as satisfying as it used to be." [20]

"I have helped many anxious patients by teaching them how to breathe. Anxiety, and breathing are so linked together that helping the one often improves the other. Some of these people have given up tranquilizers, sleeping pills, and other sedative medications after they learned how to breathe normally." [21]

As an experiment, Dr. Steincrohn found that he could actually *induce* severe anxiety states and fear attacks by having one of his

47

patients breathe rapidly and shallowly. As soon as he had her breathe regularly and deeply again, all her anxiety and fear symptoms vanished.

Thousands of years ago, Yogis developed the science of *Pránáyáma* (control of breath or vital energy) to slow the breath, lengthen the pause periods of the *pránendriya*, and thus control, calm and relax the mind. In this way, disturbing and negative emotions can be eliminated from the mind altogether. These advanced techniques are taught by trained Ananda Marga Yoga teachers, because if this subtle science is practiced improperly, it may result in great harm to both body and mind. *Pránáyáma* should *never* be practiced without the close guidance of a trained teacher.

Proper Breathing

BREATHE THROUGH THE NOSE

Mouth breathing–inhaling through the pharynx and the larynx (throat)–allows air to reach the bronchial tubes without being properly filtered, moistened and warmed. In order to be cleansed of dust and bacteria, air should be drawn in through the nasal passages where mucus membranes with their secretions filter it, and where the germicidal properties of these secretions kill many of the incoming bacteria. In this way also, the air travels a longer road, and in the journey it is warmed to the body temperature, instead of being allowed to hit the vital organs with a chilly shock. Breathing through the mouth is an invitation to colds and infections of all sorts.

Perhaps most important, however, is the fact that breathing correctly through the nose creates the proper subtle energy flow through the channels of vital energy which end in the nose (*idá* and *piungala*, see page 60).

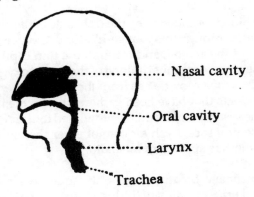

Nasal cavity

Oral cavity

Larynx

Trachea

EXHALE DEEPLY

The lungs are spongy, porous tissues, extremely elastic and containing innumerable sacs. When we breathe, air passes in through the nose, down the trachea or windpipe (which is in turn subdivided into innumerable smaller tubes called bronchioles) and into the many small air sacs (alveoli) of the lungs.

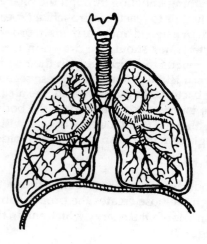

The blood, pumped in by the right side of the heart, circulates continuously through this sponge-like lung. Oxygen penetrates the thin walls of the alveoli, and through the thin capillaries into the blood. The air sacs are thus drained of their pure oxygen and in turn filled with carbon dioxide gas from the blood, generated from the waste products that have been gathered up by the blood from all parts of the system. Unless this accumulated foul air is squeezed out from these tiny sacs, fresh air cannot enter them, no matter how much strength is applied in inhalation.

In ordinary breathing we only squeeze air out from the middle and upper portion of the lungs, and the base of the lungs lie

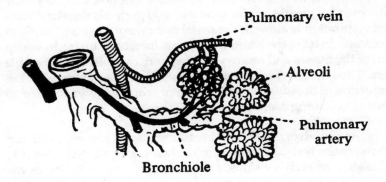

Pulmonary vein

Alveoli

Pulmonary artery

Bronchiole

almost inactive, filled with stagnant air. "Altogether the lung has a volumetric capacity of about five liter of air. Of these, only about three litres are ventilated, that is, inhaled and exhaled at each deep respiratory act, whereas a liter to a liter and a half are never ventilated, and stagnate in the lung, totally unused."[22]

This imperfect exhalation or emptying of the lungs allows a considerable part of the lungs to remain inactive, and such portions offer an inviting field to bacilli, which attack the weakened tissues. According to medical reports, tuberculosis is due principally to lowered vitality, due to insufficient supply of oxygen. Good, healthy tissue will resist attack, and the only way to have good, healthy lung tissues is to use the lungs properly by expelling all foul air and refilling them with fresh air.

This is one of the reasons that Yogic breathing emphasizes long, slow, deep exhalation, so that as much as possible of the old stagnant air can be removed and replaced with fresh air. The more air is squeezed out, the more fresh air rushes into the lungs from the atmosphere. By careful breathing, the exhaling period may be gradually increased following slow and deep inhalation, while the respiratory rest in between inhalation and exhalation is extended in proper proportion. In time, the ventilation rate becomes very slow (down to 8-9 breaths a minute or less) and perfectly regular. When the respiration is slowed, the metabolic rate of the body tends to decrease. In turn, the heart, having less metabolic toxins to sweep out of the tissues and less oxygen demand, may allow itself a little rest. Thus the rhythm of the heartbeat is reduced along with the reduction of breathing from 70 beats per minute down to 40 or 30 during breathing exercises.

As a result of this slowed breathing there is less wear and tear on the entire body: less work for the heart, lower blood pressure, relaxation of body tensions, and quieter nerves. A feeling of extreme peace arises in the mind and body, with no air hunger whatsoever.

CIRCULATION AND RESPIRATION

From the lungs, oxygenated blood travels to every cell in the organism. Without this supply of oxygen, the tissues would quickly die. Not only does the blood bring oxygen and nutrients to the cells, it also carries away waste products back through the veins. All of the blood in the body makes this trip every three minutes. Without proper respiration and circulation the body simply cannot function efficiently. As one doctor explained, "In the absence of sufficient oxygen, the metabolic fires burn low, like a fire with a poor draft. Instead of glowing with life, the poor breather is cold, dull and lifeless. He or she lacks warmth and energy." [23]

What happens to the cells without a proper supply of oxygen? The tissues age and cannot properly regenerate, and digestion and elimination of waste materials and toxins are greatly hindered. The brain needs three times more oxygen than the rest of the organs, and when it does not receive enough, thinking processes are slowed, in the same way that the mind becomes sluggish in an ill-ventilated room. Without any oxygen at all, the brain cells die in four minutes.

During the practice of ásanas and breathing exercises, the breathing becomes deep and slow and the lungs are expanded to their full capacity; as a result the body and mind receive all the oxygen and vital energy they need. Fatigue vanishes and one feels filled with radiant inner energy.

BREATHE DEEPLY, DIAPHRAGMATICALLY

Inspiration occurs when the expansion of the chest and lungs creates a slight vacuum in the chest cavity, causing air to be drawn in. This expansion of the chest is created mainly by the diaphragm, aided by the pull of the small muscles between the ribs and the muscles of the shoulders.

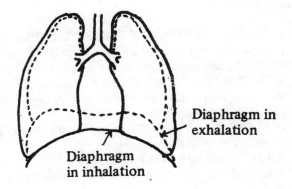

Diaphragm in
exhalation

Diaphragm
in inhalation

The diaphragm is a large dome-shaped muscle separating the chest cavity, containing the heart and lungs, from the abdominal cavity. During inhalation the diaphragm contracts and flattens, pushing down on the abdominal organs. Whether your diaphragm moves properly or not can easily be discovered by watching the movement of your abdomen: when the diaphragm is contracted, the abdomen should protrude. If the abdomen is already tense and contracted, the diaphragm cannot properly descend.

Most people breathe incorrectly, using mostly the chest and shoulder muscles; but in yoga practice one learns to breathe diaphragmatically, using the large diaphragm muscle to totally ventilate the lower lungs, and squeeze out all the stagnant air.

Thus *the science of breath control starts with the proper control of the diaphragm* and the respiratory muscles of the chest and shoulders. The lungs should be expanded to their maximum, to absorb the greater amount of life-giving *prária* from the air.

A HEALTHY VENTILATION OF THE LUNGS IS ATTAINED WHEN THERE IS:

1. AN ERECT POSITION OF THE VERTEBRAL COLUMN with the rib cage held in a relaxed upright position, in order to avoid compression of the lungs, heart and other organs.
2. A DEEP SLOW INHALATION first using the diaphragm as a sucking pump, then expanding the rib cage with the help of the rib and shoulder muscles
3. A SLOW EXHALATION using mostly the diaphragm in reverse action as a squeezing pump
4. A REGULAR BREATHING RHYTHM
5. A REGULAR VENTILATORY REST after exhalation. [24]

Yoga and Old Age

The result of the average individual's pitiable waste of human energy and potential is that a person becomes old before his or her time. Today's fast-paced and artificial life has enormously quickened the wear and tear of the human body. Improper posture tightens ligaments and tendons and leads to impaired respiration, backache and headache. Impaired respiration–shallow breathing and a sluggish diaphragm–results in poor oxygenation and poor digestion, with all their ills. Lack of proper exercise causes stiff muscles, ligaments and joints, arthritis, and obesity. Improper diet also results in obesity, as well as hardening of the arteries, high blood pressure, and heart disease. The skin loses its resilience, elastic tissues degenerate, and wrinkles form all over the body. Anxiety and worry upset the system with one emotionally-caused disease after another. The body stiffens, dries out, and gives up.

Yogic asanas and breathing, as we have seen, cleanse and stimulate the human body in every way, improving and regulating metabolism, harmonizing glandular secretions, burning up fat, limbering joints, stimulating circulation, improving digestion, liberating increased energy–in effect, rejuvenating the organs and systems of the body. Thus the yoga practitioner always looks–and feels–young.

> "For those who have conquered the body through self-control, through the fire of Yoga, there is no disease, no old age, nor death."
>
> Svetasvatarpanisad

Instructions

DO NOT STRAIN OR HURRY

Naturally we don't all start out able to practice ásanas perfectly, like the illustration in asana books. As you practice ásanas, do so realistically in terms of your own body. Approximate the form as best you can and still be comfortable in the pose, able to hold the pose for the minimum count.

Straining has no place in ásanas. Overexertion can cause injury that may keep you out of practice for a long time. The elderly and those unaccustomed to daily exercise should take up ásanas in a most gradual manner. Ásanas are different from western sports and calisthenics, modern dance and ballet, so even those accomplished in those fields should begin their practice carefully. One should not do ásanas after a major operation until completely recovered and no pain is felt (unless otherwise directed by your teacher). Whenever you feel the slightest pain while performing the asanas, STOP IMMEDIATELY and relax until recovered. Always rest in *Shavásana* (Dead Pose) between postures until you feel your heartbeat and breathing return to normal. At the end of your ásana practice, you should feel fresh and invigorated, not exhausted! Working harmoniously in this way with your own nature, after a short time of sincere, careful and consistent practice, you will soon see for yourself your increased strength, flexibility and energy.

While forcing the body is completely contrary to the nature of ásanas, so is laziness and under-doing a pose. Between these two extremes is single point of challenge, at which the posture is comfortably sustained and the physical capacities are inspired to stretch and grow. Through this sustained pressure the secretion of the hormones is affected. *Do not jump in and out of asanas,* hurrying from one to the other. It isn't how many you do that matters, it's how thoroughly you do them. Go slowly. Delight in the motions of this marvelous machine of the Divine, your human body. Let your mental wanderings find rest in the rhythmic pulsation of your breath. . .And after a time, as you release the posture to rest and enter another, feel that the flow of your movement is sustained by the flow of your breathing. Move with such presence of mind and such grace that you feel your poses becoming steps in a cosmic dance.

PRACTICE ASANAS TWICE A DAY

Particularly those who are doing meditation should practice asanas twice daily, after morning and evening meditation, when the mind and body are relaxed and inspired. By practicing asanas twice daily, the body is both prepared for the day's activities and calmed for the night's rest. Each time you should practice at least four asanas, followed by massage and deep relaxation. After relaxation, do not do any strenuous activity or exercise; try to spend a few minutes alone, in silence—or go for a walk alone—to enjoy the inner tranquility gained from the asana practice.

...WITH A CLEAN AND RADIANT BODY

Before the practice of asanas or meditation, you should always do "half bath" (soap is not necessary, and in cold weather you may use slightly warmed water):

1 – Pour cool water on the genital area
2 – On the legs from the knees down
3 – On the arms from the elbows down

4 – Holding water in the mouth, splash water on the open eyes, 12 times
5 – Do "nose drink": hold a little water in the palm of your hand and tilt your head back and pour this water gently into your nose; then spit it out of your mouth.
6 – Wash your mouth with water and clean your throat with your middle finger.
7 – Wash the ears and behind the eras.
8 – Wash behind the neck.

This practice cools the body, relaxes the heart and nerves, and calms the mind, thus preventing many diseases. Even in cold weather, certain parts of the body become overheated from continual activity, and their nerves are almost constantly stimulated–especially the face and hands, feet and legs, and genital organs. By the half-bath, these overheated parts of the body are cooled and the functioning of the entire nervous system is improved.

Half bath should always be performed before those activities which heat the body (meditation, ásanas, meals, and sleep), to cool the body first before performing them. By splashing cool water on the arms and legs, the blood vessels in these areas are contracted, and the blood is redirected to the brain, heart and internal organs. Thus before ásanas, half bath relaxes the nervous system and sends more blood to the internal organs and glands, to stimulate their proper functioning; before meditation, it supplies extra blood and energy to the brain for easier concentration. Before meals, it improves the appetite and gives extra blood and energy to the digestive organs. It also relaxes the mind (see below) before eating for better digestion, and prevents over-acidity (dyspepsia) caused by emotional tension. Before sleep, it calms the mind and induces a sound, deep sleep.

EYE SPLASHING: Splashing water on the open eyes has many benefits. By washing dirt and dust from the eyes, it strengthens the eyes and improves the eyesight. It also gives mental clarity, for the eyes are connected directly to the brain, and thus cooling the eyes cools the brain also. When one is feeling lethargic or drowsy at work or study, half bath—especially eye-splashing—will bring about immediate alertness and recharged mental energy.

Splashing the eyes has another immediate benefit which scientists have recently discovered. Splashing cool water on the face automatically slows and regulates the heart beat, due to a reflex action called the "diving reflex".* Many doctors are now using this face-splashing technique to treat heart patients.

"NOSE DRINK": Due to improper diet, mucus or phlegm may collect in the sinus cavities in the head and make one easily tired, lethargic and susceptible to colds, especially in winter. The "nose drink" clears this mucus out of the sinuses, thus preventing colds and making the mind clear and alert.

The half-bath should be practiced regularly to maintain health; because of its relaxing effect on the body and mind, it has been called one of the "secrets of longevity."

* * * * * * * * * * * * *

Whenever possible you should take a full bath before doing ásanas so that during the massage you will rub the natural oil back into your clear skin (see page 81), instead of surface dirt and toxins like urea excreted by the cells. However, do not bathe for at least 30 minutes after ásanas, to avoid washing away these same oils; and also because the body becomes slightly heated from the ásana

---

* The "diving reflex" is a vestigial reflex in humans inherited from our aquatic ancestors, whose nervous systems were programmed to redirect the body's energies inward when diving into water.

practice and bathing immediately may cause chill or cold. It is advisable not to come in direct contact with water at all for ten minutes after the deep relaxation pose.

A cold bath before ásanas takes the sluggishness out of the muscles and clears the pores so that the skin can absorb plenty of oxygen.

BREATHE THROUGH THE NOSE

Breathing through the nose not only filters, moistens and warms the air reaching the lungs, but it also promotes the proper flow of vital energy in the body. Throughout the practice of ásanas, always try to breathe deeply and gently through your nose.

KEEP THE LEFT NOSTRIL OPEN

There are two main channels of vital energy of *prána* in the body, which weave around the spinal column and end in each nostril (*idá* and *piungala* in Sanskrit). The five lower cakras are located at the intersection of these energy channels. When the breath is flowing predominantly through the left nostril, the body remains cool; this is the most conducive time for profound thought, meditation, or ásana practice. When the breath is flowing predominantly through the right nostril, the body

---

* Underarm hair and hair of the legs should not be removed, since it not only regulates body temperature and preserves body heat, but also affects the delicate hormonal balance of the endocrine system.

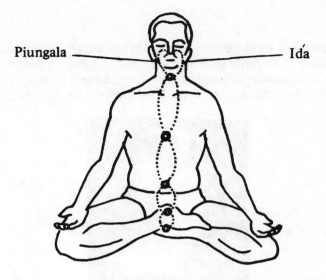

Piungala ——————————————— Ida

becomes more heated and the mind and body are prepared for physical activity in the material world.

Thus the breath should always be flowing through the left, or both, nostrils at the time of ásana practice. If the left nostril is blocked, it may be opened in the following ways:

1)   Lie down on the right side of your body, resting your right ear against the innerside of your upper arm. Remain still until the left nostril opens. (Lie on the opposite side to open the right nostril).

2)   Sit up straight. Pull the left heel in towards the body, and the right knee in towards the chest with the foot flat on the ground. Lean the right armpit onto the right knee. As you breathe, sustain the pressure of the armpit on the knee until the left nostril is open.

PRACTICE IN FRESH AIR AWAY FROM DRAFT

There should be sufficient fresh air in the room where ásanas are practiced, but no draft should come in contact with the body, to avoid muscle spasm, stiffness and other discomforts caused by chill. Ásanas should never be practiced outside or in a completely open place, for the rapidly varying temperatures of the outdoors may also cause chill.* Nor should they be practiced in direct sunlight, for sunlight dries up the precious natural oils stimulated by the asanas. These oils should instead be conserved and rubbed back into the skin (see Massage, page 81). Always practice ásanas on a blanket or mat, never on the floor.

---

*   If it is necessary to go outdoors after practising ásanas, and if the body is still heated or it is cold outside, sufficient clothing must be worn to prevent catching cold. While going outside, inhale while still inside the room and exhale as you go out, to prevent any vibrational shock of changing temperatures on the nervous system.

The room where asanas are practiced should always be free from dust, trash, and noxious fumes from smoking, gas stoves, spray deodorants, etc. All of these interfere with proper breathing.

WEAR SUPPORTIVE UNDERWEAR

Asanas should be performed whenever possible in private, wearing only a minimum of clothing. Supportive underwear (underwear for men, and bra and underpants for women) should be worn to avoid accidental muscle strain. No tight clothing like belts should be worn which would restrict ease of movement. Tights and leotards should also not be worn because they absorb the precious natural oils secreted by the skin. Rings, bracelets, watches, etc. should be removed, and pens and any sharp objects should be taken out of the pockets.

The fingernails and toenails should also be kept short, to avoid pressure or scratching of the nails on the body during the practice.

NEVER PRACTICE ASANAS DURING MENSTRUATION

Asanas should never be performed during the menstrual period to avoid excessive bleeding or irregular menstruation. However, *Padmásana* (Lotus Pose) and *Viirásana* (Brave Pose) may be performed during menstruation also *Shravásana*(Dead Pose) and certain mild warmups which do not bend the body at the waist, as well as, of course, massage and meditation.

In order to prevent menstrual cramps, women should regularly practice *Yoga Mudrá* (Yoga Pose) and *Diirgha Pranám* (Long Salutation, page 76 and 77). A major cause of cramps is the straining of the transverse muscles of the back due to the heavy accumulation

63

of excess fluid inside the body. These two ásanas, practiced regularly, strengthen these back muscles and greatly diminish the discomfort of menstruation.

Ásanas should not be performed after the fifth month of pregnancy; they may again be resumed one or two months after giving birth. During the entire period of pregnancy, however, concentration, Dead Pose, and massage should be practiced. In fact, deep relaxation is very important for the pregnant mother, because the state of her mind has a profound effect on the embryo; throughout the pregnancy she should practice regular meditation to keep her mind in a perpetually peaceful state.

PRACTICE ON AN EMPTY STOMACH

The best time for ásanas is in the morning before breakfast and in the evening before dinner. Ásanas should not be performed two-and-a-half to three hours after meals, for practising asanas during digestion may result in stomach ache, nausea and indigestion.

Do not eat or drink for one-half hour after ásana practice; for eating too soon after asanas disturbs the subtle benefits of the ásanas on the glands, muscles, circulation and vital energy flow. It is also desirable, as the body becomes more and more subtle from the regular practice of ásanas, to eat a pure vegetarian diet.

The Ásanas

There are many ásanas, about 50,000 including all the variations, invented by yogis to affect different glands and *cakras*, and thus to affect the mind and body in various ways. Many of these are being openly taught in the hundreds of yoga books available in bookstores everywhere. But it must be emphasized that *it can be very dangerous to practice ásanas without the close guidance and instructions of a trained yoga teacher.* One cannot know the subtle effects of ásanas on the body, or which postures to choose in order to correct the imbalances of body and mind. Everyone's glandular constitution and flow of vital energy is different, and everyone's mind is at a different state of consciousness. Thus ásanas must be prescribed like specific medicines, *individually,* by an experienced teacher. Practising ásanas on one's own from a book is like taking powerful medicines without the guidance of any doctor.

The following ásanas will not only maintain physical health but will rectify various defects in the endocrine glands thereby removing the disturbing emotions and mental imbalances which may hamper concentration. Not all of these are necessary for everyone; one's particular asanas should be taught by Ananda Marga Yoga teachers in individual consultation. *No one should risk harm by practicing asanas without the guidance of a trained teacher.*

SHOULDERSTAND (SARVÁUNGÁSANA):

Lie down on your back. Gradually raise the entire body and keep it straight, resting its weight on your shoulders. The chin must be in contact with the chest. Support both sides of your trunk with your hands. The toes must remain together; the eyes must be directed at the toes. Practice three times, from one to five minutes each time.

Dr. Steven Brena explains the benefits of this posture in his book, *Yoga and Medicine:*, "There is a dual mechanism of stretching and isometric contraction of three distinct muscular groups – stretching of the back muscles, contraction of the muscles in the abdominal wall, and contraction of the fore muscles of the neck.

This stretching of the back muscles leads to a reduction of basal tension of these muscles, with the elimination of many muscular stiffnesses resulting from a poor orthopedic position of the vertebral column. The contraction of the abdominal muscles restores an often neglected functionality to them and at the same time eliminates the fat stored in the abdominal walls.

"With the contraction of the fore muscles of the neck, coupled with the pressure of the chin on the chest, there is a redistribution of the blood in the upper part of the trunk, with important results. For, while arterial circulation to the brain remains normal through the vertebral arteries, the arterial thrust in the carotids and the venous deflux of the jugulars are slowed down. Consequently, the thyroid, the thymus (in the young) and the parathyroids receive an increase in blood flow, which stimulates and improves their function. Modern endocrinology teaches us that the thyroid gland is a star of the first magnitude in the endocrine constellation, so much that its deficiency causes cretinism (stunted growth). An improved thyroid function, therefore, is translated into a general well-being for the entire human organism."

FISH POSTURE (MATSYAMUDIRÁ):

Lie down in *Padmásana*. Rest the crown of the head on the floor and grasp both the big toes with the hands. Practise three times. Maximum time for practice is two-and-a half-minutes.

67

This asana should always be practiced as a complement to the shoulderstand and must be held for half as long as the shoulderstand. The eyes should be viewing the tip of the nose.

TWIST POSE (MATSYENDRASANA):

Press the Muládhara Cakra with the right heel. Cross the left foot over the right thigh and keep it to the right of the thigh. Grasp the left big toe with the right hand, keeping the right arm along the left side of the left knee. Reach backwards from the left side with the left hand and touch the navel.

Turn the neck to the left as far as possible.

Then press the *Muládhara* with the left heel and reverse the process. One round comprises completing the process on both sides.

Practice four rounds, each round lasting for half a minute.

BRAVE POSE (VIIRÁSANA):

Kneel down and sit on the heels. Bend the toes downwards. Rest the backs of the hands on the thighs, the fingers pointing towards the groin. Direct the vision at the tip of the nose. The Yoga teacher will give directions as to the duration of this asana.

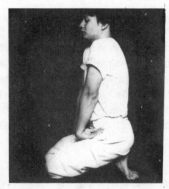

WHEEL POSE (CAKRÁSANA):

Lie in a supine position. Flex the legs to bring the lower legs in contact with the thighs. Both the hands will rest close to the shoulders. Supporting the weight on the soles and the palms, raise

the head and the trunk. The body will assume the shape of a wheel in this ásana. Duration–half a minute. Practise four times.

BOAT POSE OR BOW POSE (NAOKÁSANA OR DHANURÁ-SANA):

Lie in a prone position. Flex the legs to bring the lower legs close to the thighs. Directing the hands over the back, grasp the ankles. Raise the entire body, supporting the weight on the navel. Extend the neck and chest as far back as possible. Look toward the front. Breathe in while raising the body and maintain yourself in that state for eight seconds. Resume the original posture while breathing out. Practise the ásana eight times in this manner. The body assumes the shape of a bow during this ásana.

FULL HEAD-TO-KNEE POSE (UTKATÁ PASCIMOTTÁNÁ-SANA):

Lie in a supine position and extend the arms backwards, keeping them close to the ears. Rise while exhaling and insert the face between the knees. Make sure that the legs remain straight. Grasp both the big toes with the hands. Remain in this state for eight seconds. Now resume the original posture while inhaling. **Practise eight times in this way.**

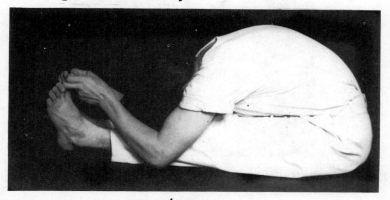

PLOUGH POSTURE (HALÁSANA):

Assume the position of *Sarváungásana* (Shoulderstand). Gradually bring the legs backwards and extend them as far as possible. Let the toes of both feet touch the ground. Keep both the hands in a prone position on either side of the body. Duration—as in **the case of Shoulderstand.**

PERFECT POSE (SIDDHÁSANA):

Press the Múládhára Cakra with the left heel. Then press the Svádhisthana Cakra with the right heel. Place the hands palm up on the respective knees. Duration–as long as you wish.

LOCUST POSE (SHALABHÁSANA):

Lie down on your chest. Stretch the hands backward with the palms upward. Raise the legs and the waist, keeping the fists clenched. Duration–half a minute. Practise for times.

COW'S HEAD POSE (GOMUKHÁSANA):

(i)   Sit down and extend the legs forward. Bring the right leg under the left thigh, placing the right foot under the left buttock. Now bring the left leg across the right thigh and place the left foot under the right buttock. Place the left hand on the spine. Then bring the right hand backward over the right shoulder and interlock the fingers of the hands in a chain-like fashion. Duration-half a minute.

(ii)   Practise in the same way with the left leg under the right leg. Completing this on both sides constitutes one round.

Practise four rounds.

BALANCE POSTURE (TULÁDANDÁSANA):

(i)   Standing on the left foot, direct the other foot backward and raise it. Grasp the waist on either side with the respective hand, and then bend the trunk and the head forward such that the head, the trunk and the leg (extended backward) are parallel to the floor. Duration–half a minute.

(ii)   Standing on the right foot, repeat the process.
Practise four times.

HEAD-TO-KNEE POSE (JÁNUSHIRÁSANA):

Press the Múládhára with the right heel. Extend the left leg forward. While exhaling, touch the left knee with the forehead. Then, interlocking all the fingers firmly, press the left sole with the hands. There should be complete expiration when the forehead touches the knee. Maintain this position for eight seconds. Separate the hands and sit erect, while breathing in. Then press the Múládhára with the left heel and repeat the above process exactly. One round comprises practising once with the left and once with the right leg. Practise four rounds.

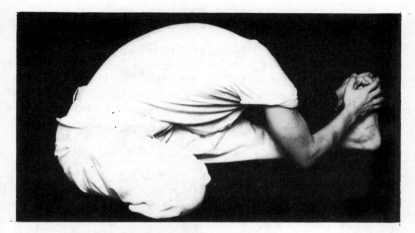

PEACOCK POSE *(MAYURASANA):*

Assume a squatting position. Bring the wrists together and place the palms on the floor, with the fingers pointing towards the feet. Now bring the elbows in contact with the navel and stretch the legs backward. Supporting the weight on the elbows, raise the head and the legs from the floor. Duration—half a minute. Practise four times.

COBRA POSE *(BHÚJAUNGÁSANA):*

Lie down on your chest. Supporting the weight on the palms, raise the chest, directing your head backward. Look at the ceiling. Breathe in while rising, and after having risen, hold your breath for eight seconds. Come down to original position while breathing out. Practise eight times. (This is an excellent ásana for women.)

YOGA POSTURE *(YOGAMUDRÁ):*

Sit in Bhojanásana (with legs crossed). Pass both hands backward and grip the left wrist with the right hand. Then bring the forehead and the nose into contact with the floor, breathing out during the process. Maintain this state for eight seconds and then rise up, breathing in. Practise eight times. (This is another excellent posture for women, especially for menstrual problems.)

LONG SALUTATION (DIIRGHA PRANÁMA):

Kneel down, and, holding the palms together extend the arms upward, keeping them close the the ears. Then bend forward in a posture of bowing down, touching the floor with the tip of the nose and the forehead. The buttocks must continue to touch the heels. While bending down breathe out, and stay in a state of complete exhalation for eight seconds. Then rise up, breathing in. Practise eight times. (This is an excellent ásana for women, especially for **those suffering from menstrual trouble.)**

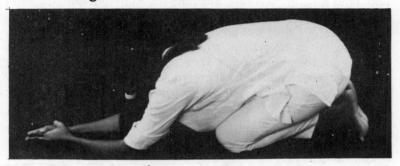

HARE POSE (SHASHÁUNGÁSANA):

Kneel down and grasp both the heels firmly. While exhaling, bring the crown of the head into contact with the floor in a posture of bowing down. The forehead should touch the knees. Maintain this posture for eight seconds, holding the breath. Breathe in while rising. Practise **eight times.**

HAND-TO-FOOT POSE (PADAHASTÁSANA):

Stand erect, raising the arms, palms open. Then bend the trunk and the left arm leftwards while breathing out, and in a state of full expiration touch the left foot with the left hand. After maintaining this position for eight seconds, raise the body and extend the left arm upwards, breathing in throughout the process. When the body is perfectly erect again, bend the trunk and the right arm rightwards, breathing out, and, in a state of complete expiration, hold for eight seconds, touching the right foot with the right hand. Then raise the trunk, extending the right arm upwards, inhaling throughout the process. Then bend the trunk forward, breathing out in the process, and catch hold of the big toes. Stay in this position for eight seconds. Then, breathing in, rise up, and raise the arms and extend them backward. When you cannot bend any farther back, hold yourself in that position for eight seconds, retaining the breath. Then bend forward while breathing out, and,

just touching the big toes (i.e., without staying in that position), raise the trunk and the arms, breathing in. One round is then complete. Practise eight rounds, making sure that no part of the body below the waist is bent at any time.

UTKSÉPA MUDRÁ

The following is a very good exercise to improve digestion, especially for those who are normally constipated. Chronic constipation is a very dangerous condition and may cause many more serious diseases. Due to constipation the toxins and waste materials of the body, instead of being excreted, accumulate and are reabsorbed into the blood, thus poisoning the entire system and causing many illnesses. So it is essential that the bowels should be moved at least once a day: those who have sluggish digestive system should perform this *mudrá* everyday without fail.

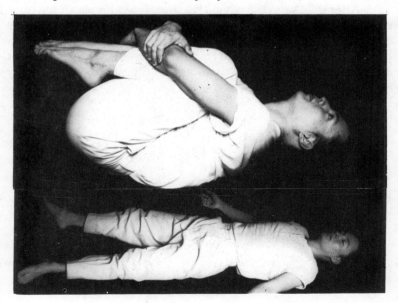

As soon as you wake up in the morning, while still lying in bed, inhale deeply and flex both your legs, pressing them tightly against your chest with your arms. Then vigorously extend the legs out straight, exhaling completely. Repeat about 6-8 times.

Then rise and drink a full glass of water. Doctors say that drinking a full glass of water immediately upon arising is one of the best ways to stimulate the peristaltic motion of the intestines and activate a sluggish digestive system. It is better if you add a little fresh lemon juice and a pinch of salt to the water. This will reduce the acidity in the stomach and blood, which is a cause of many digestive troubles. Be sure to clean your mouth before drinking because many digestive poisons collect in the mouth during the hours of sleep; this is why we awaken with a bad taste in our mouth. Thus it is preferable to drink the water without letting it touch the teeth.

After this, keep the naval area uncovered for about ten minutes. The naval area (*Mánipura cakra*) is the energy center for digestion; by exposing it to the *prária* (vital energy) in the fresh morning air, it becomes strengthened. The regular daily practice of this mudrá will relieve constipation, and digestion will be greatly improved.

Massage

A'sanas should always be followed by massage, for massage is the ideal finish to the revitalizing practice of asanas. A'sanas stimulate the sebaceous glands which lie under the surface of the skin to secrete their natural oils. These oils are the most perfect skin balm for the human body. The massage returns these beneficial secretions back into the skin, thus keeping it soft and supple. To conserve these natural oils, a'sanas should be performed away from sunlight, and a bath should not be taken for thirty minutes after the massage.

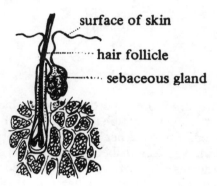

surface of skin

hair follicle

sebaceous gland

Massage also stimulates all the nerve endings at the surface of the body, thus stimulating the entire nervous system, and it harmonizes the "aura" of pranic energy which surrounds the body. It relaxes the muscles to a very low basal muscular tension; it enhances the blood circulation, thus helping to prevent infection in case of injury; and it promotes all-around health.

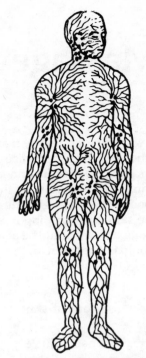

The Lymphatic System

Massage has one more important benefit which concerns the flow of lymph in the body. Lymph is a vital fluid which purifies the blood, thereby enhancing the health and beauty of the body. This clear fluid fills the spaces in between the cells and the blood capillaries, and acts as a "go-between" for the blood and the tissues. It picks up dead cells and waste matter and then flows back in lymphatic vessels toward the heart. But before the lymph rejoins the blood, the waste matter is filtered out at large lymph nodes, where white cells eat the wastes and carry them to the spleen. There they are broken down into fragments small enough for the kidneys to dispose of.

This purifying lymph is not moved along the lymphatic vessels by the pumping pressure of the heart, for it is a separate system entirely. Rather it moves in its slow course solely by the action of the muscles. Massage greatly stimulates and facilitates the flow of this lymph and thus the purification of the blood. Special care should be taken to massage the areas of the important lymph nodes—neck, armpit, groin and knee. In the massage on the following pages, these areas are emphasized.

At the end, the feet are carefully massaged. Many of the body's nerves have nerve endings in the feet, and thus massaging the feet stimulates the flow of nerve energy throughout the internal organs (see Foot Chart, page 92). In this way, the massage completes the stimulation of the internal organs, blood, lymph, glands, and the relaxation of the skin and muscles, and prepares for' the deep relaxation of the Dead Pose.

MASSAGE TECHNIQUE

(1) Massage up the forehead and over the top of the head, and down the back of the head with the palms, three times.

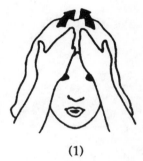

(1)

(2)

(2) With the tips of the fingers, massage out a across the eyebrows, three times.

(3) With the pointer finger press down in the crease between the top of the eyeball and eyebrow. (Pressure on this spot stimulates the vagus nerve to slow down the heart; thus it calms and relaxes the body and prepares for the deep relaxation pose.) Continue pressing with the fingers, moving with the fingers, moving them across the top of the eyes, down the temples and around the ears. Repeat three times.

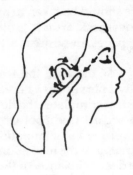

(3)

(4) Twist the pointer finger gently into the ears. (Fingernails must be short for this.).

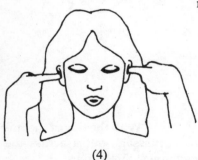

(4)

(5)   Rub hands together briskly until they become slightly warm. Close the eyes and press the base of the palms gently over the closed eyes. Relax completely and breathe deeply. Do this three times.*

(5)

(6)

(6)   With the outside edge of the palms, massage from the sides toward the tip of the nose. Do it three times.

(7)   With the tips of the fingers, massage under the eyes and down the sides of the face: then turn the hands sideways and massage across the sides of the head to the back of the neck, finally massage the neck from the front to the back with the palms. Repeat three times.

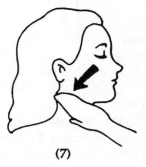

(7)

* This is very good for the eyes, especially for eyestrain. Those with poor eyesight should frequently "palm" their eyes in this way, and also rotate the eyes slowly in all directions – left and right, up and down, diagonally and rotating in clockwise and counter-clockwise circles, always relaxing and "palming" the eyes after each exercise.

(8)　Massage　"moustache" area from center to sides of the lips with the tips of the fingers, three times

(8)

(9)

(9)　Massage down the cheeks, starting by massaging the upper sides of the face with the heels of the palm, then sliding the hands down while massaging, so the tips of the fingers meet at the chin. Repeat three times.

(10)　With the two thumbs, massage up inside the jaw starting under the chin and outward toward the sides of the face, three times. (This massages the lymph nodes and salivary glands in the neck.)

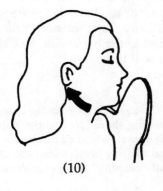

(10)

(11)

(11) With the two heels of the hands pressed against the center of the neck, massage outward to the sides of the neck. (This pressure on the center of the neck affects the vagus nerve and lowers the blood pressure and the heartbeat as in (3), thus relaxing the body very effectively.) Repeat three times.

(12) Raise the left arm and massage down the left armpit with the fingers, three times. (This massages the lymph nodes under the arm.)

(12)

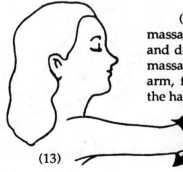

(13)

(13) With the right hand, massage over the left shoulder and down the upper arm. Then massage around the lower forearm, following the direction of the hair.

(14) Massage the top of the left hand, and the palm; rotate around each finger. (Do not pull them out or crack them.)

(15) Repeat 11, 12, and 13 with the right arm.

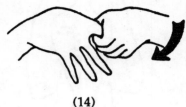

(14)

(16) Reaching up over the right shoulder with the right arm, and down behind the back with the left arm, bring the two hands together in the midback (as close together as possible). Now massage upward with the right hand and downward with the left hand, thus massaging the spine. Do three times. Reverse the hands and repeat.

(16)

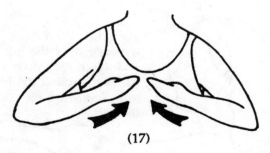

(17)

(17) Massage the chest, by rubbing in toward the heart with both hands.

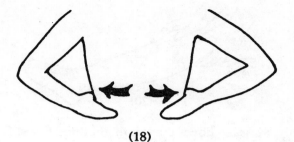

(18)

(18) Exhaling, place thumbs at the sides of the body and fingertips at the base of the rib cage, and massage out to the sides of the body with the fingertips, three times. In this way, exhaling and massaging out to the sides, work down the front of the body until you have massaged the trunk of the body from the waist all the way down to the legs. This massages all the internal organs.

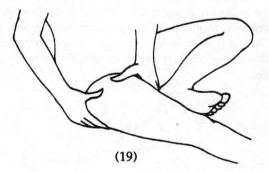

(19)

(19) Encircle both hands around the joint of the body where the left leg meets the trunk, and massage this juncture. (Many lymph nodes are located here.)

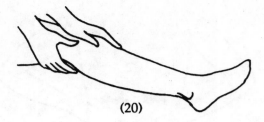

(20) Massage down the left thigh, three times. Follow the direction of the hair growth.

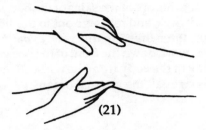

(21) Place the right palm over kneecap, and curl fingers around the kneecap. Place left hand under kneecap and massage with a combined motion of these two hands, wiggling the kneecap around. This, and all the joint massages, helps prevent arthritis and rheumatism in the joints; it also massages the lymph nodes located at the knee.

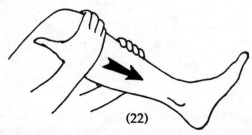

(22) Massage down the calf, following the direction of the hair growth.

(23) Massage left ankle: encircle the ankle with the fingers so that the thumbs meet at the ankle bone on the inside of the foot. Rub around protruding ankle bone.

(24) Massage left foot, top and sole, with the thumbs.

Gently twist and squeeze each toe. Stretch toes apart and massage in between the toes. Press your fingers in at the juncture of the toes and foot. Knead foot with thumbs, massaging sensitive areas with a gentle circular motion. Make knuckles with your fist, and press the knuckles on the outside edge of the foot, drawing them down from the toe to the heel firmly, three times ... then from the center of the foot to the heel, three times. Slap the foot with the palm, gently. Rub the sole of the foot.

(25) Repeat with the right leg.

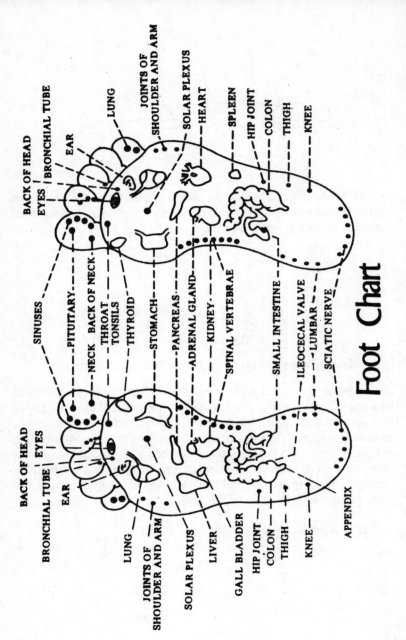

Foot Chart

BACK OF HEAD
EYES
BRONCHIAL TUBE
EAR
LUNG
JOINTS OF SHOULDER AND ARM
SOLAR PLEXUS
HEART
SPLEEN
HIP JOINT
COLON
THIGH
KNEE

SINUSES
PITUITARY
NECK BACK OF NECK
THROAT TONSILS
THYROID
STOMACH
PANCREAS
ADRENAL GLAND
KIDNEY
SPINAL VERTEBRAE
SMALL INTESTINE
ILEOCECAL VALVE
LUMBAR
SCIATIC NERVE

BACK OF HEAD EYES
BRONCHIAL TUBE
EAR
LUNG
JOINTS OF SHOULDER AND ARM
SOLAR PLEXUS
LIVER
GALL BLADDER
HIP JOINT
COLON
THIGH
KNEE
APPENDIX

92

TANDAVA

Tandava was introduced as a spiritual dance 7,000 years ago by the great Indian yogi, Shiva, who was also known as Nataraj (the Lord of Dance). The word tandava is derived from the Sam'skrta word 'tandu', meaning 'jumping' Tandava is the fundamental step, 'the primordial pace', of all oriental dance.

The dance is performed by vigorous jumping from one foot to the other, the knee of the raised leg crossing one of three selected points-the navel, the heart, or the throat.

Danced twice a day at the end of meditation or ásanas, for a period of 5 minutes, tandava represents the struggle between the forces of life and death. Accordingly, the arms extended hold symbols traditionally associated with each: in the right hand (representing the life force of the sharpened and vigilant mind) a knife, sword or trishula (3 pronged spear) and, in the left hand (representing the fear of death) a snake, skull or fire. Tandava develops the heart and mind of the true spiritual warrior, who possesses firm determination to struggle against and conquer all forms of fear, and even death itself.

The spirit of tandava is expressed in the sentiment "I will face the fear of death, which surrounds me on all sides, and overcome it with the power of the life force of my mind. No force will deter me from the goal. No evil tendency, no enemy, no bondage can shake my determination to be victorious."

This vigorous dance, performed individually, as well as collectively, is intended for men only, since it has a masculinizing effect: it stimulates the adrenal cortex which secretes male hormones. These hormones in turn stimulate the testes to produce testosterone, the hormone responsible for 'maleness', i.e. secondary male characteristics; in comparison to women, more body hair, lower voice, enhanced development of skeletal muscles and

93

bones, and a greater degree of agression. Tandava also stimulates the entire circulatory system, the heart, and lungs–and also the muscles of the feet, lower leg, thigh, pelvis, back, neck and arms. Tandava thus reduces the possibility of heart attack, high blood pressure and lung atrophy. More importantly, tandava is the only physical activity that exercises the brain. Thus, tandava is an indispensable spiritual practice for developing virility, vitality and courage.

1) Stand on the toes, arms stretched out to the sides.

2) The heels of the feet kick the back of the thighs while jumping up; land on the toes in squatting position.

94

3) Bring the knees to the chest while jumping up, stand-erect.

4) Stand on left leg, jump up and swing right leg sideways to the left.

5) Same as (4) on the other leg. Carry on the dance, increasing the speed.

6) Standing position.

7) Jump into squatting position and stand up.

95

KAOSHIKII

Kaoshikii comes from the Sam'skrta word 'kosa' meaning "sheath" or layer of the mind: this dance which is especially for women, develops not only the body but the subtler layers of the mind.

The dance is performed by raising the folded hands directly overhead, in a vertical position. The body is bent 3 times to the right and then 2 times back to the original position (upright). The upper part of the body is kept straight, from the waist to the fingertips, with the arms straight at the elbows and the middle fingers always touching. The lower part of the body keeps rhythm with the arm movements by stepping to left and right, touching the ball of the foot to the ground behind the heel of the other foot.

The final part of the dance is performed by vigorously stepping 2 times in place, stamping the heels firmly on the ground.

Kaoshikii is beneficial for the entire body, from head to toe. It keeps the spine flexible, reduces unnecessary body fat and promotes regular menstruation. By reducing pain during delivery, it eases childbirth. Depending on the individual, it can be danced even during menstruation and until the sixth month of pregnancy.

Kaoshikii also increases longevity, keeping the body fit even until the age of 80. It stimulates the heart and circulatory system, and creates suppleness in the joints knees, hips, spine, shoulders. Kaoshikii is thus an invaluable health practice, especially for women, for it develops strength, flexibility and endurance, and by its stimulating effect on the spine and nervous system, it strengthens and sharpens the mind as well.

Baba   **Nam**

Baba   **Ke**   **valam**

Baba   **Nam**   **Baba**

97

Keva   **lam**   **Baba**

Nam   **Baba**   **Baba**

Nam   **Baba**   **Ke**   **valam**

Deep Relaxation

To the question, "What do you attribute your
long life to?" The most frequent reply of very old
people is, "Freedom from worry."

Modern life is a perpetual race against time. Business pressures, hurried meals, over-stimulating entertainments, improper
food indulgence in alcohol and drugs, continual emotional tension
and anxiety – all are taking their toll in nervous indigestion and
fatigue, restless sleep, strain and irritability, as well as all the
myriad other psychosomatic illnesses that beset modern humanity.
Today's human being has completely forgotten how to relax.

Watch a person who states, "I am relaxed," and note his or her
position, almost always spread all over the armchair or bed he or
she is "relaxing " in. His or her disorderly attitude, even in its
seeming stillness, involves multiple muscular tensions whose total
adds up to an enormous unconscious and inefficient muscular
labour. Even in sleep, people often toss, strain and perspire, according to the rhythm of their uncontrolled dreams. Thus the normal
person's muscles are rarely at rest: even during sleep, we spend a
great deal of physical and mental energy.

As one doctor said, "All of this, translated in terms of human
economy, means a great waste of biological energy." Through the

At the present stage of evolution, human beings are little aware of the pranic forces, and consequently heavily identify themselves with matter, deluding themselves into thinking that they are the body. They also forget that matter is nothing else but condensed energy in continuous transformation. They waste vital energy to feed their senses with a variety of stimulations, born out of an unending chain of material desires. The more they dwell on matter, the more they need "fleshy" nutrition to keep themselves alive, and the more they "burn." The more they burn out oxygen, the less they feel the pranic forces within themselves, and the more they sink into matter.

Dr. Steven Brena

nervous pathways a continuous amount of vital energy flows from the inside toward the outside, fading unused into the environment. The average human being is an absolutely anti-economic machine requiring a great quantity of fuel to supply a very limited work: his or her muscles are engines which "heat" both while they run and while they rest.

"All of this happens in the normal individual; but if emotional factors interfere, the consumption of energy climbs sky-high and can go bankrupt, burning and wasting all one's vital resources. How many liver diseases, upset stomachs, heart ailments and headaches are caused by this foolish waste of energy?" [25]

STRESS AND ADRENAL GLANDS

The effect of stressful emotions on the body and mind is now being carefully studied by scientists, as more and more people all over the world fall ill and die due to stress-related diseases. In a stressful situation, the adrenal glands automatically secrete hormones like adrenaline, which mobilizes all the organs of the body for extreme exertion to either fight or flee (see page 13). This instinctive response is a legacy of our primitive past; for when our early ancestors faced dangerous situations they dealt with them in bursts of intense physical exertion until the stress was over–either fleeing rapidly from predatory animals or clubbing an enemy into unconsciousness. But contemporary human beings can neither flee from their problems nor physically battle their adversaries, and thus they face continual and unrelenting stresses which they cannot respond to with physical activity.

The employee who is constantly criticized by his boss, the student under constant pressure of excess homework and exam deadlines, the harried housewife, all build up intense inner tensions. Emotions like anger send shock waves through their nervous

Primitive human beings could release the inner tension of stressful situations by physical activity; modern humans must keep it bottled-up inside.

systems and their muscles tense, their breath becomes irregular, and their fists clench. Their blood pressure increases, their hearts race, and their digestion is impaired. But although they are prepared for a burst of activity, they cannot physically release this tension by hitting someone over the head or running away, so they bottle it up inside. Their overstimulated adrenal glands maintain their bodies and minds in a state of perpetual alarm and inner tension, and as a result they develop melancholy, depression and anxiety neuroses, even as early as grade school. This prolonged stress depresses the immune system and lowers the resistance to infection and disease, and thus often results in many disorders such as hypertension, heart disease, stroke, bowel disease, stomach ulcer, asthma, migraine headache, arthritis, and even cancer. Drugs to reduce tension have been found to have disturbing side effects. To relieve our debilitating inner tensions, *we must learn how to relax.*

THE ART OF RELAXATION

Watch a baby asleep on a bed. It gives up its weight entirely to the bed, without any muscular tension.

Nomadic peoples all over Asia, journeying night and day, reach an oasis or camping place and at once throw themselves on the ground and lie there limp, apparently lifeless from head to foot. One hour of this rest refreshes them with as much new vitality and energy as a night's sleep for the average person. These wanderers are able to undertake surprisingly long journeys with very little rest.

Babies and primitive people have not yet forgotten the art of relaxation, the ability to completely rest at will. This art has been practiced by yogis since ancient times. They began their experimentation on this state by watching animals in deep relaxation during sleep, and especially during hybernation.

103

During even a few minutes of deep relaxation, there is a rapid fall in blood pressure and pulse rate, and the strain on the heart is reduced. The overtaxed nerve centers are revitalized and muscle tension drops even below the basal muscular tension level. Since during deep relaxation only a very small amount of vital energy is being consumed, the remaining energy which is being constantly

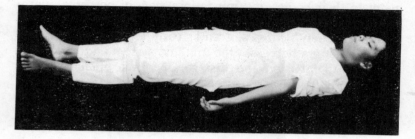

produced by the cells of the body can be conserved and accumulated for future needs. Disturbing emotions and worries dissolve from the mind. The whole body is thus reinvigorated in the shortest possible time; and many ailments, especially those due to nervous tension, may be relieved completely. In one experiment, 47 hypertensive patients performed deep relaxation daily for several months. Their headaches, nervousness, irritability and insomnia completely disappeared, and their blood pressure was lowered to normal. [26]

"Yoga practitioners do not need to go on vacation to relax. They can remain seated in a room open to the traffic of a busy metropolis and can transform themselves to the point that they hear no sounds, being relaxed and quickly self-possessed on a chair, just as if they were in a green Swiss valley. Translated into medical language, this capacity of voluntary sensory-motor inhibition is achieved through a gradual and conscious inversion of biological current: no longer a flux from the interior to the exterior, but a flux from the exterior to the interior.

"To give an example, again taken from electricity, yoga practitioners can voluntarily put themselves in the position of a telephone or radio operator who wants rest, and so switches off all the contacts of his or her sets; impulses still reach the sets, but are no longer perceived and, therefore, do not disturb the operator. Lying thus in a state of perfect and conscious peace, yoga practitioners can, through respiration, connect themselves with pranic energy. Now they are like batteries put into contact with a source of electrical energy in phase of continuous charge, whereas a common person is like a battery working continuously, unable to recharge itself."* [27]

POISE IN ACTION

When this deep relaxation is carried over to the state of activity, the muscular reflexes respond more rapidly to stimuli and every task can be performed more efficiently, more effortlessly.

A cat crouches before a mousehole, gracefully motionless. It exhibits tremendous strength and vitality in repose. The machinery of action is not strained in waiting, but all is ready...and when it darts forward, action burts like a flash of lighting from its stillness.

Every genius consciously or unconsciously relaxes during the process of creation, and for this reason is so efficient in his or her art. Contrast this poised grace to the movements of today's hurried businesspeople, who with their exaggerated, wasteful movements, fidget and fume, and wear themselves out before the hour for action has arrived.

---

* This drain of vitality and wear-and-tear of the body due to stressful emotions has been actually photographed by Kirlian photography, as we have seen, which reveal the bright flares of energy streaming from the fingertips of an emotionally tense person (see page 38).

Through the regular practice of deep relaxation, yoga practitioners develop the ability to keep their minds and bodies in perfect equilibrium in all situations. Learning how to relax and maintain "grace and pressure" in this age of rapid change– when high blood pressure and heart disease are the number one killers in technological societies–is one of the most valuable abilities of human life.

DEAD POSE

Shravasana or "Dead Pose" can be done anytime, even at times when most other asanas are prohibited, such as during sickness, menstruation, or pregnancy. In this pose, the body remains completely motionless and becomes recharged with pranic energy, and the mind's attention is gradually withdrawn from the body and surroundings to be absorbed in a state of deep inter tranquility. The body and mind together attain a perfect blissful repose.

To receive the complete benefit from the practice of asanas, the Dead Pose should be performed for about ten seconds to one minute between each posture. The proper rest in Dead Pose completely calms the body and prevents the over-straining of muscles and the over-stimulation of the glandular, circulatory and respiratory systems. One should rest at least until the breathing and heartbeat have become calm. Asanas and massage should always be followed by the deep relaxation pose for at least three minutes. Those with high blood pressure should do at least five or ten minutes of deep relaxation daily; for as we have seen this is one of the best treatments of hypertension.

When you perform the Dead Pose, lie down on your back, covering yourself with a sheet if you feel a chill. Stretch the arms and legs gently apart and turn the palms up; the fingers will naturally curl in. Close the eyes. Do not move a muscle of your body, even your eyeballs. Remain as motionless as if you were dead. Immerse your mind in the flow of your breathing, in a state of refreshing peace.

Relax your feet and your toes. . . . your calves, knees and thighs
. . . . feel that both your legs are completely relaxed–there is no tension or pressure anywhere. Now relax all your internal organs–
your digestive system, your lungs, your heart. . . . relax your back
and spine. . . . Now feel your fingers: relax your fingers and hands,
your wrists, your lower arms and elbows, your upper arms and
shoulders, and your neck. . . . Now you should feel that your entire
body from the neck down is completely relaxed; there is no tension
anywhere.

Feel that flow of relaxation now moving up into your face,
relaxing your cheeks, your mouth and lips, your ears, your nose,
and your eyes–feel all the tension around your eyes completely
dissolving–your forehead and head are completely
relaxed. . . . Feel your brain inside your skull. . . . your brain is also
completely relaxed. Now your whole body from the tips of your
toes to the top of your head, is completely relaxed. You feel as light
as a feather, and very comfortable.

Now be aware of your breathing. Breathe slowly and deeply,
from the diaphragm. As you inhale, imagine that you are inhaling
cosmic energy into every cell of your body; your mind and body are
becoming completely recharged. . . . Feel the energy from the cosmos flowing through you, washing away all the tensions and
negativity, cleansing you inside and out. . . . Feel yourself full to
overflowing with this purifying energy, radiating from every pore
of your body. . . . filling your whole being with joy and love. . . .

Remain in this position for as long as you like. Afterwards you
will feel completely refreshed in body, mind and spirit.

Meditation

If, as we have seen, due to the subtle interdependence of mind and body, mental attitudes play a significant part in our getting sick, they can also play a "significant role in our getting *well.*" Human beings have an astonishing capacity to *enhance* the efficiency of their immune systems, and thus their level of health, by *positive ideation.* Positive mental attitudes in a state of self-relaxation can reduce pain and relieve many illnesses including high blood pressure, chronic headaches, and even paralysis and asthma.

The amazing effect of "placebos"–simple sugar pills given to patients who are deluded into believing that they are real medicines–in relieving pain and curing diseases is one clear example of the power of the mind in restoring health. [28] And a remarkable new cure for cancer has been developed by Dr. Carl Simonton, who guides his patients to relax and *visualize* their white blood cells, like a powerful army on a "search-and-destroy mission," conquering and then carrying off the dead cancer cells. When 110 terminally ill cancer patients practiced this novel form of mental therapy, 25% *of them were totally cured of* cancer; in 30% the previous rapid growth of the cancers completely stopped, and in 10% the cancer went into remission (started to disappear.)

One of the most effective techniques for self-mastery through positive thinking is meditation. Scientific experiments have shown that the response of the human organism to meditation is just the *opposite* of its reaction to stress: it quiets the central nervous system, slows the heart rate, *lowers the blood pressure by as much as* 20% , and slows the breathing to *less than half its* normal rate. As all the body processes relax, the meditator experiences a state of profound rest, even deeper than sleep, and much energy is conserved and accumulated for later use. He or she feels a heightened alertness and mental clarity, and physical and mental efficiency after meditation techniques is greatly enhanced: for unlike ordinary rest, after which one's alertness is often diminished, meditation improves one's reaction time and motor skills.[30]

A recent study of employees of a large western company who practice meditation techniques twice a day revealed the tremendous benefits of meditation in all aspects of their lives. After only five and a half months of meditation, they reported a decrease in depression, hostility and stress, less irritability, and the disappearance of psychosomatic disorders such as colds, headaches, and sleeplessness; as a result, absenteeism was greatly reduced. The most frequently reported benefit was the ability to think clearly; those who practiced deep meditation said they felt more alert, more sociable and empathetic, and enjoyed life more than before they learned meditation. "I do not feel so defensive in my relationships with other people"...."My reasoning process is clearer, and I am better able to assign priorities and handle them in proper order"...."I can think, remember and organize better."[31]

One of the reasons for the increase in alertness and the ability to think clearly is that during meditation there is a *35% increase of blood flow to the brain.*[32] The blood supply to the brain is closely related to our mental abilities, and with the increase of blood, and the corresponding increase of oxygen, the brain's overall functioning improves. (One of the causes of senility that occurs in many older people is the *decrease* of blood flow to the brain.)

Other remarkable research has shown that although people who experience a great deal of stress in life are more likely to get sick, those who practice meditation can withstand more stressful changes in life with less illness than those who do not. In fact, the ability to handle stress increases with meditation, and those who practice meditation techniques experience much lower levels of daily anxiety. Rather than feeling helplessly tossed about by the

109

buffering waves of life, as many people do, those who practice meditation, feel in control of their lives, and less dependent on others.[33] Thus meditation is the most effective means—more effective than any drug—to reduce stress and prevent stress-related diseases. A few minutes of daily meditation completely relaxes and recharges the body and mind, filling you with fresh energy to be used for work.

INCREASED POWER OF MIND

But the greatest benefit for many people who meditate regularly has been the increase in will force. Regular meditation trains the capacity to pay attention and ignore distractions, and those who practise this, feel at the same time more relaxed and more alert, as if they were "using their brain more efficiently than ever before."[34]

Meditation is the key to success in all spheres of existence, for those who can check the restless wanderings of their minds and focus their attention at will, can learn anything easily and achieve their desired goals in life. Experiments on students have shown that those who practice meditation techniques constantly excel in their examinations due to their increased ability to concentrate and their total lack of "test anxiety."

LOTUS POSE

The proper position for meditation was carefully designed by yogis for the maximum development of the powers of meditation. In Lotus Pose (*Padmaśana*), the right foot is placed on the left thigh and the left foot on the right thigh; the hands are clasped together in the lap, palms up, and the jaws are pressed against each other with the tongue curled up, touching the upper palate. This posture puts selective pressure on the lower two cakras (*Múládhára and*

110

Svadhisthána), thus redirecting their energies upward to the brain. It also calms and controls the entire nervous system.

Experiments performed in a British laboratory revealed that persons simply sitting in this posture, not even trying to meditate experienced an immediate change in their brain waves, from the more restless and rapid beta rhythm (about 24 cycles per second) to the calmer and slower alpha rhythm (8 cycles per second), an indication of relaxed mental alertness and inner serenity.

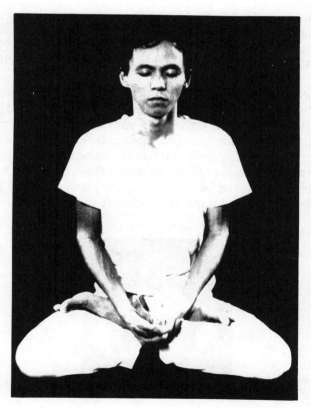

In another experiment, subjects were given math problems to solve while sitting in this position and their brain waves, heartbeat and respiration were tested. While they worked they were subject to sudden and loud noises, bright lights, and very cold objects. It was found that in this posture they reacted *much less* to those disturbing stimuli than people sitting in an ordinary position; they were able to concentrate more deeply and to solve the math problems more easily. The scientists concluded that the Lotus Pose brings about an automatic sensory withdrawal and internalizes the energy of the mind.

Thus one should sit in Lotus Pose during meditation as much as possible; even if it is difficult at first, by practicing knee exercises regularly, the tight ligaments in the thighs will soon loosen and enable one to sit comfortably in this beneficial position.

KNEE-LOOSENING EXERCISE: Sit with your legs bent in towards your body, with your feet touching. Hold your ankles and gently push your knees down with your elbows. Concentrate on loosening the stiff muscles and ligaments. Do not jerk or push rapidly; push steadily until you have stretched as far as you can, and hold that position until it feels comfortable, then stretch again. If you repeat this exercise every day, your knees will soon be able to touch the floor, and it will be very easily to flex the legs in Lotus Pose.

THE SCIENCE OF MEDITATION

The profound rest attained during meditation is partly due to the process of sense withdrawal which is essential part of meditation. Sitting motionlessly and silently with the hands and legs folded and the eyes closed, the person imagines himself or herself in a remote and peaceful environment. He or she does not see, hear, touch, smell or feel anything external, nor speak or move or work in the world. Thus all the senses and motor organs are "turned off" and the mind is completely withdrawn from the external environment.

Then, to turn off the ceaseless "chatter" of thoughts and enter a state of deep, mental tranquility, one breathes slowly and deeply, and concentrates on the peace within. This deep, rhythmic, diaphragmatic breathing stills the restless thoughts of the mind and generates such tremendous psychic energy that the mind is gradually stilled and calmed, and enters a state of serene awareness and inner happiness.*

* Further information about spiritual meditation can be found in *The Way of Tantra*, also published by Ananda Marga Publications

113

In the calm of the mind, it is the substance of the mental being that is still, so still that nothing disturbs it. If thoughts or activities come, they do not arise at all out of the mind, but they come from outside and across the mind as a flight of birds crosses the sky in a windless air. It passes, disturbs nothing, leaving no trace. Even if a thousand images, or the most violent events pass across it, the calm stillness remains as if the very texture of the mind were a substance of eternal and indestructible peace.

Yogi Aurobindo

Mastery Over Self

Dr. Jonas Salk, the Nobel prize-winning discoverer of polio vaccine, once described the critical period through which humanity is now passing as a transition from "Epoch A" to "Epoch B"– from an age of competition to a glorious new age of cooperation, from an age of "either/or"–"either *you* or *I* will survive"–to an age of "both/and"–"both you *and* I will make our lives successful." In this entirely new epoch which humankind is now entering, "holistic medicine" will be the dominant model for healing, as healers and patients alike realize that medical treatment is not the repair of ailing part of the body, but the restoration of the proper functioning of the whole being–not only of body, but of mind and spirit as well.[35]

In the past, physicians usually restricted themselves solely to the physical body and neglected or ignored the psychological aspects of illness. But this mechanistic concept of medicine is now considered simplistic, and out-of-date; doctors are becoming increasingly aware that virtually all disorders are psychosomatic in the sense that they involve a continual interplay of mind and body in their origin, development and cure. As chronic degenerative diseases proliferate all over the world–cancer, heart disease, strokes, aids, respiratory diseases, gastro-intestinal ailments, migraine headaches, backaches, arthritis–the stress-related "afflictions of civilization"– more and more people are coming to understand that to cure themselves they have not only to take medicines, but to *change the way they live.*

Centuries ago, yogis realized that we are not simply this body, but subtle patterns of life energy in constant flow and fluctuation, and that disease is the manifestation of disharmony and imbalance

115

in the body and mind. They recognized the important role of the *cakras* (the controlling points of the flow of vital energy throughout the body) as the link between body and mind, and the function of the endocrine glands to mediate between the cakras and the physical organs. Through long experimentation they developed subtle and powerful techniques of healing and health to influence the entire organism at a more fundamental level of being than simply the physical–techniques of exercise, breathing, relaxation and concentration, that are being practiced by increasing numbers of people in the world today and will be the cornerstone of the future holistic system of health on this planet. By this unified approach to the whole mind-body system,–this "psychosomatic health care,"–those who practice yoga learn to control their negative and disturbing emotions and to withstand and reduce stress. Those who regularly practice meditation as well as ásanas develop voluntary control over their internal states and their high blood pressure, heart trouble, skin eruptions, chronic headaches and pains, insomnia, asthma, and even paralysis completely disappear.

Thus, instead of becoming helplessly dependent on our physicians, addicted to painkillers, or suffering the serious side-effects of allopathic drugs, we must take more personal responsibility for our health and learn to contact, as Dr. Albert Schweitzer said, "the doctor within." By following a wholistic system of *preventive health care* that includes not only exercise, relaxation and meditation, but bathing and proper diet as well, we will maintain our entire being in perfect balance and harmony.

By the regular practice of yoga, we will become the masters of ourselves – free from disease, youthful and relaxed, full of joyful energy, flowing in harmony with the cosmos. With perfectly functioning and controlled bodies, and minds free from all emotional disturbances, calm and poised in all situations, we will be prepared and energized to perform tireless and fulfilling service in the world, dynamic activity for the welfare of all humanity.

116

One who is at peace and is quiet, no sorrow or harm can enter, no evil breath can invade. Therefore one's inner power remains whole and intact. . .If the bodily frame of a person labors and has not rest, it wears itself out. If one's vital energy is used without cessation, then it flags, and having flagged, runs dry. A purity unspoiled by any contamination, a peace and unity not disturbed by any agitation, posed and self-controlled activity which is in accord with the motions of nature—such are the secrets of an ideal life.

Chuang Tan

THE NINE SECRETS OF LONG LIFE:

1)   PROPER PHYSICAL EXERCISE

2)   TAKING MEALS ONLY ON THE URGE OF
      APPETITE

3)   GOING TO BED AS SOON AS ONE FEELS
      SLEEPY

4)   FASTING AT INTERVALS

5)   REGULARITY IN YOGA PRACTICES

6)   HALF-BATH BEFORE YOGA PRACTICES
      SLEEP AND MEALS

7)   EATING YOGURT AND RAW FOODS

8)   GETTING OUT OF BED VERY EARLY
      (BEFORE DAWN)

9)   FOLLOWING THE SIXTEEN POINTS.
      (THE SPIRITUAL PRACTICES OF
      ANANDA MARGA)

FOOTNOTES

1. Albert Szent-Gyorgi, "NRTA Journal," 1982.
2. *Brain-Mind Bulletin,* August 1978.
3. Drs. Barbara Betz and Carolyn Thomas, *Johns Hopkins Medical Journal,* May 1981.
4. Fritjof Capra, *The Turning Point* (Simon & Schuster, New York 1982).
5. *Brain/Mind Bulletin,* November 1979.
6. Dr. Harold Streitfeld.
7. Experiment by Dr. Lennart Levi, Stockholm, Sweden, 1971.
8. Marilyn Ferguson, *The Brain Revolution,* Bantam Books, 1975, page 225.
9. Dr. Steven Brena, *Yoga and Medicine,* 1972.
10. *Ibid.*
11. *Ibid.*
12. *Ibid.*
13. Sheila Ostrander and Lynn Schroeder, *Psychic Discoveries Behind the Iron Curtain,* Prentice Hall, Inc. Englewood Cliffs, New Jersey, 1970.
14. *Ibid.*
15. *Ibid.*
16. *Ibid.*
17. Vivekananda, *Raja* Yoga, Ramakrishna Mission Publications, Calcutta.
18. Research of Dr. Valery Hunt of UCLA, California, USA, as described in *Human Behavior* magazine, January 1979.
19. Swami Vishnudevananda, *The Complete Illustrated Book of Yoga.*
20. Dr. Peter Steincrohn, *Cosmopolitan* magazine, February 1973.
21. *Ibid.*
22. Dr. Steven Brena, *op cit.*
23. *Ibid.*
24. *Ibid.*
25. *Ibid.*
26. K. Datey, *Angiology,* Vol. 20, 1969, pages 325-333.
27. Dr. Steven Brena, *op. cit.*
28. Norman Cousins, "Medical Mystery of the Placebo," *Saturday Review* October 1, 1977.
29. Fritjof Capra, *op. cit.*
30. John White, *The Frontiers of Consciousness.*
31. Daniel Golene, "Meditation Helps Break the Stress Spiral, in *Psychology Today,* February 1976.
32. Dr. Ronald Jevning, Professor of Medicine at University of California Medical Center.
33. *Brain/Mind Bulletin,* July 15, 1979.
34. *Ibid.*
35. *Brain/Mind Bulletin,* September 1979.